Made in Yorkshire

# Made in Yorkshire: second to none

Maurice Colbeck

with photography by Simon Warner

 Springfield Books Limited

First published 1992 by Springfield Books Limited,
Norman Road, Denby Dale, Huddersfield HD8 8TH,
West Yorkshire, England

First edition 1992

British Library Cataloguing in Publication Data

Colbeck, Maurice
Made in Yorkshire: second to none
I Title
390.09428

ISBN 1 85688 031 1

Cover design: Douglas Martin Associates
Inset design: Etchell and Ridyard, Ilkley
Typesetting: Letaseta, Burley-in-Wharfedale
Printed and bound in Hong Kong by Colorcraft Limited

## Photography

The author and publishers would like to thank the following
for providing additional photographs:

Cochrane and Sons for the photograph on page 92 (inset)
North Yorkshire County Library for the photographs on pages
10 (inset) and 18 (lower)
Smith Settle for the photograph on page 56
The Sutcliffe Gallery for the photograph on page 75
Terry's of York for the photograph on page 22
Theakston's Brewery for the photograph on page 66 (top)
Whitby Literary and Philosophical Society for permission to
use the photograph on page 79

All other photography is by Simon Warner


Cover photography

front: the drystone waller at work in the shadow of
Kilnsey Crag
back: a York glazier at work

frontispiece: the Tuesday market at Hawes

# Contents

# Introduction

## A county of many skills

'I like work – I could watch it for hours,' – the old joke may be a little time worn, but behind its flippancy there hides an unchanging truth. For most of us have an avid curiosity about the next man's method of earning his bread, especially if the end product is something we find interesting or beautiful, or if the making of it calls for skills handed down for centuries.

Every land has its heritage of working skills and, like the products themselves, these are to a great extent the consequence of local geography. Thus Norway's coastline, her fjords and forests and long dark winters, have fostered in her people their skills as seamen, ship builders and woodcarvers. But counties, as well as countries, have their skills, both modern and traditional, and Yorkshire's share is rich indeed. Furthermore, this county – England's largest – with its hills and dales, market towns and industrial cities, vast acres of farmland bordered by a long coastline, is perhaps the most varied in England. And inevitably that variety is echoed in the products of its people.

So between the covers of this book are the stories of cheese and chocolate, beer and books; of jet carving on the coast, ropemaking and drystone walling in rural areas. You will meet clogmakers on the fringe of industry as well as the 'little Mesters' of Sheffield's great cutlery trade. You will wonder at the richly glowing stained glass of York, admire the fine furniture of 'Mousey' Thompson's craftsmen on the northern moorlands and meet men who build ships for both peace and war on the bank of an inland river.

For this is not another book about country crafts, though Yorkshire has its full share of both crafts and craftsmen, and many of them figure in these pages. It is, rather, a book about some of the products – rural and urban, utilitarian as well as decorative – which, through the skill, hard work and enterprise of the men and women who made them, have added lustre to the name of Yorkshire.

Ancient skills are often involved: monks of the now ruined Jervaulx Abbey, for instance, knew the secrets of making Wensleydale cheese; the glaziers of York still employ skills known for centuries and Thompson's craftsmen have, in a sense, made an ancient tool, the adze, their own. Yet today the aid of the most modern methods may also be invoked: the glaziers, for example, use ultra-sonic vibrations to shake the dust of centuries harmlessly from delicate medieval glass. Even the drystone-waller, whose tools have probably changed least of all, employs a big-wheeled pick-up to carry loads which once had to be transported by man or animal power.

Developments like these do not always please visiting sentimentalists. They are apt to feel somehow cheated if an electric motor now performs some of the tasks of the 'little old man' they expect to find toiling in the manner of his forebears. Yet craftsmanship dies hard, though it may change its form. Purely manual operations are inevitably being replaced more and more by mechanical processes. Terry's of York, founded in 1767, is now a leading exponent of technology in chocolate manufacture, yet, I was told the human palate is still needed for the vital task of tasting cocoa samples, while skilled packers 'can beat the best robot' and also perform a valuable quality control operation as they work.

The selection of trades, crafts and industries for inclusion in this book has not been easy. Few of the products are entirely exclusive to Yorkshire, though in many cases the county can claim a pre-eminence in their manufacture – Sheffield and cutlery, for instance, are practically synonymous; York has certainly an honoured place in the worlds of both stained glass and chocolate. Books have long been printed and bound in Yorkshire; clogs have not only been worn but made here on a vast scale.

Some products deserve to be included on the grounds of uniqueness: many would claim, for instance, that there is no cheese like Wensleydale and no other 'mouseman' like Bob Thompson. Whitby jet is said to be the best and certainly there has never been a jet industry to compare with that which flourished in this old fishing port towards the end of the nineteenth century, when 1500 were employed in 200 workshops.

Frank Meadow Sutcliffe, photographer of nineteenth century Whitby, has left us a study of twelve men at work in a Whitby jet workshop, while a boy tends the fire in a stove. The mechanisation which made possible the development of the industry is already in evidence from the pulleys, belts and shafting which conveyed power to the grinding and polishing wheels. All the workers have their heads covered against the all-pervading dust from the grinding of the jet, but there is no apparent safeguard against the deadly danger of dust inhalation.

Perhaps when we regret the passing of old ways of working we should remember that the progress we sometimes disparage has also brought increased safety to the workers who, by hand and brain, minister to our needs and our pleasure and 'maintain the state of the world'.

Maurice Colbeck

## Acknowledgement

I am indebted to many people for their co-operation in the researching of this book. In most cases their names will be found in the following pages. Unfortunately it is not possible to mention individually every one of the numerous friendly people who, again and again, have turned aside from their work to give me an insight into their particular skills. Meeting them has been a privilege and an education: I hope they will regard this book as an acceptable tribute.

# Rope held the Dales together

Ropemaking in the Dales

Hawes! its name means a mountain pass, and time was when it had only giants for company – hills like Great Shunner, Stag Fell, Wild Boar Fell and flat-topped Addleborough which was once a summer camp for Roman soldiers based at the fort called Virosidum. Hawes claims to be the highest market town in Yorkshire, and is certainly **the** market town of Wensleydale, a distinction that was claimed by nearby Askrigg until the construction of a turnpike road brought the outside world to Hawes.

What Hawes's future might have been without the turnpike who can say, but with its tup [ram] sales, its inns and other attractions for farmers, it was clearly the place for craftspeople in the days when farming needs ensured a ready trade for a variety of products. So with the turnpike came prosperity and people. At the beginning of this century Hawes was humming with rural industries, accommodating no fewer than: fourteen tailors, four women's dressmakers, twelve joiners, besides cobblers, milliners, a printer, a clock repairer, blacksmiths, cabinetmakers, plumbers and tin-smiths, a saddler and a ropemaker called William Richard Alfred (or Billy Dick) Outhwaite.

Billy Dick Outhwaite came in 1905, having decided that he could no longer make a good enough living from farming at Stalling Busk, where his family first settled in the 1730s. His son, Tom Outhwaite, now turned eighty, still lives in Hawes and is hardly more than a good rope's length from the ropeworks. He and his rosy-cheeked, smiling wife Laura had been out for a walk in the early December sunshine when they found me waiting on their doorstep after visiting the works which still bear his father's name, though they've been under different management since 1975 when Tom retired and the business passed to Peter and Ruth Annison.

How did Tom feel about the way the business had changed? 'In my time I was just making things for the farmers', he said. 'At this time of year, for instance, I'd be making hay creels for carrying hay to the sheep on the fells. And when January got turned I'd be making rope traces for the mowing

*Above: Tom Outhwaite – a life-long ropemaker*

*Inset left: Billy Dick Outhwaite seated at the big wheel spinning the warps with which to make yarn for webbing. The warps stretch the length of the rope-walk (c. 1941)*

machines and sledges.' Now, he admits without rancour, 'Visitors play a much bigger role in the ropemakers' fortunes.' Even in Tom's day visitors arrived 'wanting to see ropes made', but at best they were a distraction from his real work.

By comparison with those times, farmers now use very little rope. 'When the tractors came on to the land, it hit my business very hard. Until then, everything had been pulled up by horses. Before my father died, at 81, he wanted me to pack up. "You're

*Ruth and Peter Annison*

*Hawes and the River Ure from the north*

flogging a dead horse'', he used to say.' Harsh words to Tom Outhwaite who was making ropes when he was ten years old. It was hard and monotonous work, but his ready chuckle as he recalls the hard-old-days shows that he has no regrets.

But there are aspects of the business that Tom would hardly recognise today. The present owners, Ruth and Peter Annison, were both college lecturers when they decided that they would like to buy the ropeworks. The Press made the most of what they called the 'drop-out teachers' who had opted for the peace and quiet of country life, but in truth, though neither was Dales-born, both were seasoned visitors to the area. Peter is a Yorkshireman hailing from Leeds, while Ruth comes from Wensley – that's Wensley in Derbyshire, not Wensleydale.

One day, in the summer of 1974, Ruth happened to call in at Outhwaite's works with no more business in mind than the purchase of some skipping ropes. Arriving at coffee time, she was soon in conversation with Tom, who mentioned that he would like to sell the business. Ruth was immediately interested, and Peter, a textile chemist, was no less so. 'We'd been contemplating a move up here, and this seemed to be as near to textiles as you could get.' Soon, the Annisons were the new owners of the Outhwaite ropeworks, though they were wise enough to retain the company's time-honoured name. Tom entered a thoroughly well-earned

*Above: a rope in the making*

*Left: twisting machine*

retirement, while remaining always ready, if called upon, to offer advice or practical help.

'It was an incredible change', recalls Peter, of the transition from twentieth-century technology to traditional rural practice. The only concession to modernity at the ropeworks when they took over was an electric motor on the twisting machine. Otherwise, little had changed in a century. And it is a demanding calling, as Ruth found out: 'If you make rope all day, you walk eight miles – that's the equivalent of walking the Pennine Way every six weeks without the hills.'

The traditional ropemaking process still employed at Hawes consists basically of four stages. Stage one, warping up, involves two pieces of equipment, one known as a twisting machine on which four 'crooks' [hooks] are arranged in a diamond pattern, and the 'sledge' on which a single hook is fixed centrally. The sledge moves on runners (hence the name), because the distance between it and the twisting machine is determined by the length of the rope to be made – known as the rope-walk. The strands (there may be two, three or four) are attached one to each crook on the twisting machine, and to the single hook on the sledge at the other end ready for twisting. During the twisting process, the strands of yarn are turned into a single length of rope; the sledge moves forwards as the strands are shortened by the addition of twist.

Stage two occurs when, in order to regulate and concentrate the degree of twist, the strands on the twisting machine end are kept apart for as much of the process as possible by means of a grooved wooden 'top' held by the ropemaker, who is stationed in front of the sledge and moves forwards with it as the twist is inserted – stage three.

Turning a handle at the back of the sledge adds the 'backtwist' which is inserted to 'balance' the rope so that it will not snarl up, and this completes stage four. Since 1978 one of the three ropemaking machines has incorporated a device which puts in the backtwist automatically.

The equipment which came to the Annisons with the business, included an old hand loom which at one time had been used for making cattle neckbands and Yorkshire halters, 'fairly complex things which had to be woven', Peter explained, 'but we never used it and now it's in the museum' (the Dales Countryside Museum behind the ropeworks). There was also a hand-operated twisting machine for making twine, which was equally superfluous and followed the hand loom into the museum.

'When we took over', Peter told me, 'our first requirement, having a family to support, was to increase the turnover, which meant that we had to find additional markets, and probably new products. At that stage we could afford neither new buildings nor new machinery, so we started off by making things we could sell to visitors, who were coming into the ropeworks in relatively small numbers, largely because of television programmes or newspaper publicity sparked off by the change of ownership.'

This new development went so well that the Annisons decided they could not produce adequate stocks single-handed, so they took on part-time staff who worked at home, making, for instance, macramé plant hangers. 'It's difficult to imagine it now', said Ruth Annison, but nobody knew what macramé was in the 1970s, when it was just coming in from Canada and America. At first Peter and I made macramé plant hangers at home in the evenings to sell in the shop next day. We bought pots from the local potter to put in them so as to be able to offer a complete product. Then we began to make skipping ropes as well.

'It's hard to recollect how tiny the number of visitors was in the mid-seventies. It was the James Herriot television series that really put this part of the world on the map. There had always been some visitors, from 1878 when the railway came to Hawes, but in the early days we had never considered tourism as part of the business, and yet without it we would have been in very great difficulty. The retailing provides an instant income, because when things are sold over the counter, the customer pays on the spot.'

With a shrewd and perhaps newly discovered business instinct, Ruth studied the visitors who found their way into the shop, noting their comments and asking questions about their preferences. But for all her commercial acumen, she lives in the Dales because she loves the countryside which first attracted her there. She and her husband are eager to conserve rural life and to preserve their own way of life. Whilst she would be the last to underestimate the importance of visitors, both to the ropeworks and the Dales, she recognises all too clearly that there is a dilemma in attracting them without causing some threat to the very things that they go there to enjoy.

How many of the products which filled Tom Outhwaite's working life occupy the Annisons today? A few, such as cow ties, 'though we make a mere trickle compared with the number produced in the mid-seventies', said Peter. And the trickle will probably dry up entirely due to EC legislation which may make tying up cows over the winter illegal. 'The work that Tom did, which we have continued', said Ruth, 'is done because it's still commercially valid, not in any sense because it's quaint. We're lucky that visitors regard it as an attraction. We don't use traditional methods just because they're old, but because with some products it's still the best way. Short ropes, for instance are more economically made by the old method. We still make a fair number of halters but we've actually added to the range of Tom's agricultural ropes. We now make a lot of horse lead ropes.'

Even so, ropes, which once were Outhwaite's staple product, now represent only a minor proportion of the works' total manufacturing range. 'Whereas Tom was dealing directly with small farmers, we are often catering for customers a long way from here.' Peter adds, 'We make leading reins, for instance, in the colours of twelve European countries, but we've had to diversify out of equestrian products, because it's a fairly limited market. We had to choose whether to stick with ropemaking and look for different markets for ropes or to look at the agricultural and equestrian market and decide whether or not to add a whole range of non-rope type products – things like horse blankets and numnahs [saddle cloths]. We finally decided we were best-suited to making ropes so it was a question of additional markets.'

Ropemaking at Hawes has become a more colourful operation since the Annisons arrived; in

*Norman Chapman sets up the warp knit braider*

*Above: the home of good rope*

*Left: in the early days the outdoor rope-walk was behind the workshop. Hawes church is in the distance.*

Tom Outhwaite's time, very little coloured yarn was used. Now they use a huge range of colours and, said Ruth: 'once you've introduced colour, customers want a choice'. A local housewife arrived with a consignment of church bell ropes, one of the lines into which the Annisons have diversified. Her job, she explained, was the insertion of the colourful 'fluffy bits' – the sallies – in the handles. There are no more than four makers of church bell ropes in the country, and Outhwaite's have a proportional share of this very limited market.

There is a big and growing mail-order market in the barrier ropes, used to facilitate crowd control at museums, stately homes and exhibitions and, increasingly, in banks, post offices and at airports – wherever single queuing is common. Even churches sometimes rope off the back pews to concentrate a reduced congregation at the front.

Braiding is another new departure, which has led to the production of things like dog leads. Generally, over a million metres a year of braiding is produced. It is a market the Annisons would like to explore: 'We've added a lot of braiding machinery', said Peter, 'and would have added more but until we get our new factory built, we haven't space for it.'

Amid all this change, one thing that remains constant, along with the Yorkshire skill it epitomises, is the sign reading 'WR Outhwaite & Son, Ropemaker' over a door that admits you to the premises. 'The bit you see at the front', Peter explains, 'is part of a wooden building erected in about 1923. That was extended frontwards slightly and given a brick front gable-end with a door in it. There was also a building behind measuring about thirty-five feet by twelve, feeling its age and jolly cold in winter. That was the total premises – an area of about four hundred square feet in which ropes were made, all the raw materials stored – everything. Within eighteen months of coming here, we had added an extension at the back which virtually doubled the size. Then, a few years later, we doubled it yet again by adding an extra length of building and then added on another fifty per cent, so that by now we've approximately five thousand square feet of building. We are about to start on another development stage, a building of about five thousand square feet, so we will be doubling up again.'

The total workforce, including Ruth and Peter, numbers twenty-two, plus one or two students in the summer. On the premises there are both full- and part-time workers and the total includes home workers. All are employed the whole year round. 'This is part of our policy and commitment', said Ruth, 'though it can make difficulties for us due to seasonal variations.' They have also to cope with employment regulations and the conditions peculiar to operators in a National Park.

Ruth and Peter each have their clearly defined roles. He brought to the enterprise his technical knowledge of textiles and in addition, says Ruth, has equipped himself to deal 'quite brilliantly' with the financial aspects. Reciprocally, Peter points out that the shop and advertising which take up much of Ruth's time are 'essential parts' of the business. 'Manufacturing in the UK is extremely difficult in any circumstances. To site a relatively low-technology manufacturing set up in the heart of a deeply rural area is doubly difficult and if we hadn't had the income and relative profitability of the shop to give us the cash flow needed for new machinery, I doubt if we could have achieved anything like this amount of expansion.

In Dales terms, this is a sizeable concern; for as Ruth points out, a very recent survey shows that two-out-of-three firms in the whole Settle – Carlisle corridor are comprised of no more than five people, and many have only one.

Over the whole year, about 100,000 visitors to Hawes find their way to the ropeworks. Many of them look around in surprise at the obvious evidence of a well-managed, energetically run business and confess that what they expected to see was a solitary 'little old man' pursuing a time-honoured craft by antiquated methods and stead-fastly spurning synthetic fibres in favour of 'natural' materials that no sane climber would risk using. Such traditionalists may not realise that they are witnessing a kind of rural industrial revolution in which people with an academic or scientific back-ground apply new solutions to old problems while retaining a deep love of the atmosphere and traditions of the area they have made their home.

'The tourists who come in to see what we're doing are actually enabling us to continue the manufac-turing which provides the bulk of the jobs in the place. It's a pleasantly symbiotic existence really'. Their first serious effort to cater for the tourist interest in souvenirs was made by producing skipping ropes, button thread and twine. Then, three weeks before Christmas 1976, the Sunday

*Observer* published a feature on the skipping ropes, impressed by the fact that they were hand-made attractive and good value. 'Suddenly,' said Ruth, 'we were overwhelmed with orders. That taught us there was a market outside Wensleydale.' A hundred orders would have delighted them; in the event, there were five thousand, which, by working through the night and taking on staff, the business could process in good time for Christmas.

This success led the way for other toys with rope components, such as yo-yos, and gradually other items were added, hammocks and nightlights and candles, because candle wicks are now among the products made in the factory. Their criteria for buying stock for the shop are that the item does its job well, it's made of nice materials – natural if possible, but not exclusively so – and that 'it's really good value for money'. The stock now includes paperback books on country topics and good quality leather handbags, all under £10 each. 'Because we haven't space to stock a big range, we tend to go for black and white, big and small. So there is a choice, but not a big choice. We buy large quantities and are therefore a valued customer of our suppliers. This puts us in a good negotiating position on price and delivery and we can pass on the benefit to our customers.' Hence, the whole project is firmly based on an efficiently working factory with a harmonious, congruous image in tune with its surroundings.

The Annison's plans include finding more space to enable customers to move around more easily and a wider range of goods to be more effectively displayed. They must still be the right goods, though, with a rural or nostalgic connotation that is easy to recognise but hard to define, whether a shepherd's whistle (with which you will receive free instruction) or the cubic wooden bricks with pictures that Grandma thought had vanished with her childhood. And tying it all together (as I can't refrain from saying) is the rope that 2000 summer visitors a day may watch being made before or after they go browsing in the shop.

What of the future? 'As a small firm', said Peter, 'We are perhaps best equipped to go for the specialist markets, rather than mass production For instance, we'd probably look at making magicians' cord, which suits our type of production facilities, rather than light-pull cord, because whereas you might have millions of metres of light pulls made in a year, that market has already been largely satisfied by the very large companies.'

Adaptation, say the Annisons, is the first rule of survival. They have adapted in a sensitive, ingenious and profitable way by taking an old-established business, learning the necessary skills, retaining its original purpose as far as changing demand allows, expanding it where possible along sympathetic lines and turning its largely latent tourist potential into an educative force. And all this to the benefit of the area and, not least, to the comparatively large number of people who are employed there.

Peter and Ruth suffer sentimentalists patiently. Changes there have inevitably been, but those who regret them forget that, without change, the business would have gone and Tom's and his forebears' skills been lost. Sentimentality dies hard: even the introduction of electric power to a time-honoured process is described as 'cheating', to which Peter with a smile replies – 'The electricity that runs the motor costs perhaps two pounds a week. If you are prepared to turn a handle for that amount we'll get rid of the motor.' So far, I understand there have been no takers.

*Bell-ringers at Askrigg church try out their newly hung bells and new ropes from Hawes, April 1992*

*Terry's*

MIXED DROPS

| | | | |
|---|---|---|---|
| Nominal 4-oz. Bottles | - | - | 6d. |
| ,, 8-oz. ,, | - | - | 1/- |
| Net 1-lb. ,, | - | - | 2/- |
| ,, 2-lb. ,, | - | - | 4/- |

# From the halls of Montezuma . . .

## The sweet story of Terry's of York

Young Joseph Terry must often have pressed his nose against the window of the little shop in Bootham, York, where Mr Bayldon and Mr Berry had sold lozenges and comfits since 1767. Perhaps Joseph dreamed that one day he might join them. How lucky they were to be rulers of such a kingdom of delights! But as a farmer's son, born in 1793, Joseph would probably have been expected to follow his father on to the land.

In fact, he became an apothecary, a forerunner of the pharmacist of today – though with a much wider brief. He was expected by his customers to be something of a surgeon, a chemist, and enough of a confectioner to know how to sugar a pill. Answering his calling, Joseph opened a shop in Walmgate and in 1823 acquired a wife – Harriet Atkinson, related by marriage to the same Berry family who had an interest in the shop on Bootham. Whether this led to what followed is not recorded, but it is a fact that Joseph joined the company set up by Bayldon and Berry and in 1828 was in control of it. Four years earlier the business had moved from Bootham to St Helen's Square, and there Joseph diversified his business as apothecary, baker, confectioner and peel importer.

With the move to St Helen's Square began the triumphal advance of Terry's over the years. The business was now in the hands of the second Joseph, son of the founder, and later to become Sir Joseph. By 1862 a new factory had been built at Clementhorpe, on the banks of the Ouse, to cope with the progress of the burgeoning company whose fine sugar confectionery was renowned at home and abroad. Meanwhile it was business as usual at the busy premises in St Helen's Square, where selling occupied the 'front shop' and sweets were made at the back. This building was sold by Terry's as recently as 1981.

So far, it may be noted, there has been no mention of chocolate. Yet surely, chocolate and Terry's have always been synonymous? In fact, the company's early reputation had been founded not on chocolate but on candied peel, cakes and comfits, marmalade,

mushroom ketchup and cough lozenges, with a popular line in *Joseph Terry's Conversation Lozenges*, bearing amorous opening gambits actually inscribed on the sweet, such as 'How do you flirt?' or 'Can you polka?' Until the mid-nineteenth century, there was no such thing as 'a box of chocolates' – chocolate was known only as a drink. Then a few pioneering companies, Terry's being prominent among them, introduced boxed chocolates. Public demand for the new luxury sweet appeared insatiable. By 1920 it had become essential to extend the Clementhorpe factory and during the next ten years the palatial head office and impressive works arose near York racecourse.

With boxed and block chocolate, the pioneers were breaking new ground. Who, one wonders, had first thought of actually eating chocolate? Certainly Montezuma, the Aztec emperor, had enjoyed his cup of 'chocolat' but there is no evidence that he ever dipped into a box of *Terry's All Gold*. The conquistadors caught the chocolate-drinking habit from the Aztecs and introduced 'cacao', as it was called, to Spain. When it reached England in 1640, Samuel Pepys, always ready for something new, was delighted with his first experience of what he knew as 'jocolatte'.

Chocolate was taxed, it was expensive and, like lots of other luxuries, it was smuggled – though contemporary descriptions make you wonder what the fuss was all about! By all accounts it was a pretty greasy drink in those days, due to the presence of cocoa butter. Yet without cocoa butter we should never have had chocolate to eat.

Despite all the changes there have been, the chocolate process as we know it today still begins with a bean – the seed of *Theobroma Cacao*, a tree native to South America and grown also in parts of Africa, the South Seas and Sri Lanka. When the seed pods have ripened they are fermented: they shed their pulp and turn brown, whereupon they are dried, washed, bagged and shipped. Since the cocoa tree is small and produces only five pounds of cocoa a year, while annual world consumption has been estimated at over a million tons, it can be seen that the human race requires rather a lot of Theobroma Cacao seeds.

They may not look exciting, but stepping into the cocoa bean warehouse at Terry's you could imagine yourself on a tropical waterfront – the scent of beans from a variety of exotic locations catches your throat with a faintly acid tang. From West Africa comes the basic chocolate bean, while those that impart the essential flavour are grown in Samoa, the Caribbean or Venezuela, the home of 'the very best grade of fine-flavoured cocoa in the world'. Even so, unpredictable tropic weather makes cocoa farming a chancy business – 'always the danger of a drought or a flood.'

In York the beans are meticulously blended to produce 'the Terry flavour'. And because the flavour of no two shipments can be exactly predicted, sampling the roasted and ground beans calls for experience and the possession of a subtly trained palate on the part of the mill manager or chocolatier. And also a special vocabulary is used to describe unacceptable flavours, including such terms as 'kippers', 'whitewash', 'plum pudding', 'ham' and

*Ingredient preparation for* Countline *products*

'burning tapers'.

From the warehouse the blended beans are taken to the mill, roasted, cracked and winnowed (that is, freed from the chaff). Roasting not only dries the bean, it brings out the chocolaty taste and changes the cocoa butter to prepare it to flow. Next, the beans are transferred to the nibbing machine which isolates the small dark fragments of cocoa known as 'nibs'. Nibs contain fat which is liberated in the liquor mill and during a grinding process, the fat melts to an oil, to emerge as the unsweetened 'cocoa mass', which has been compared in appearance with 'lava from a volcano' (This was the basis of the drink known to both Montezuma and Samuel Pepys.)

Depending on how the cocoa mass is to be used, it now has added to it, in the case of plain chocolate, sugar and vanilla pod or, if destined to be milk chocolate, full cream milk and flavourings. The machinery used in chocolate manufacture is fascinating and possibly unique. The ingredients are mixed until they resemble a thick brown paste.

*Hi-tech chocolatiers study a management information system on the VDU for Terry's* Carle and Montanari *moulding plant*

The paste is conveyed into a two-roll refiner which breaks down the sugar particles. The mass is then conveyed to a batch of five-roll refiners where the rollers travel at various speeds reducing the particles further to an almost microscopic one-thousandth of an inch. This extremely thorough grinding is what gives your favourite assortment the velvety texture we all tend to take for granted. Without it the texture would be rough and grainy.

The next stage of the process is conching. These machines traditionally had a curved base similar to a conch shell with a roller giving a fore and aft movement. The chocolate is gently stirred for many hours at a pre-set temperature. During the conching stage, moisture and undesirable acidic flavours will evaporate, enhancing the flavour, and the solid particles and fat become evenly distributed so that what should emerge from the conch is a rich, brown, smooth-textured cream.

In the Enrober Department, chocolate covering and decoration is added to the various fillings – nougats, toffees, caramel, almond paste, ginger, nuts and so on; or creams, toffees and fondants produced in the Starch Moulding Department. From there, the finished chocolates are foiled, packaged and dispatched.

A detailed description of the present-day chocolate manufacture would require a book to itself. What, one wonders, would Joseph Terry, the one-time apothecary of Walmgate, make of the automated, streamlined, almost magically efficient production methods of today? Or for that matter his son, Sir Joseph, who died in 1898, having seen the firm first registered as a limited company under the name now synonymous with fine chocolates, Joseph Terry and Sons Limited? One of those sons, Thomas, who succeeded his father as chairman, did much to establish Terry's in Australia and New Zealand. Another son, by a later marriage, Frank (later Sir Francis) was company chairman for thirty-five years. Thomas's son (Sir Joseph's grandson) was Noel G Terry MBE, who was chairman in 1967, when the company celebrated its bicentenary. To mark the occasion they produced the '1767' selection enclosed in a box of classic design adorned with an original illustration of York from the time Terry's was established, together with reproductions of some of the many medals they have received for excellence over the years.

Peter N L Terry, the son of Noel G Terry, and who

became deputy Managing Director, is retired now but proud that he has been made honorary life president of the company. His interest in Terry's, its products and its people is as keen as ever. He had never felt the slightest reluctance about entering the family firm of chocolate makers which traces its history back to the reign of George III. As he says: 'I've loved chocolates from being a small boy!' In those days his parents would allow him just one chocolate after meals at home – 'I think they were afraid of spoiling me.' When he went to boarding school he must have been one of the most envied of pupils – and possibly one of the most popular.

In the splendid boardroom, as we turned the pages of an album containing brochures from as long ago as 1929 he recalled bygone products, like one of his own favourites, the Devon assortment. On every page were illustrations of the colourful boxes evoking the style of their time . . . reviving memories of days when chocolate liqueurs could only be sold through off-licence shops, but delicious assorted creams cost only five shillings a pound. 'That one had a champagne cream in, and that had lemon cream and that had strawberry', he recalled fondly.

But Terry's, one feels, did not merely make and market chocolates. They sold romance and luxury in a rich assortment of flavours and a vast variety of packagings. Assortments were their forté – 'although we did block chocolate. In fact we did all kinds of things in those days. We even did liquorice allsorts, boiled sweets and a range of sugar confectionery, such as pastilles'. They very soon

*Above: final inspection of* All Gold *chocolates before placing them in the distinctive cartons*

*Left: nutcracker packer!*

began making the Chocolate Orange, without which no Christmas could ever be complete for my son – though he would doubtless be surprised to learn that when it began life in the 1920s it was actually a chocolate apple. Alas, nobody could quite remember how the chocolate apple tasted.

A great deal has happened since Peter Terry entered the company, but his memories are still fresh and vivid. At Cambridge he had studied economics, returning to York with some eagerness in his vacations, happy 'to learn about cocoas from our experts'. After serving with the West Yorkshire Regiment during the 1939–45 war, he joined the family firm in 1946, thus fulfilling a wish cherished for as long as he could remember.

Peter's father, Noel, was the last Terry to hold the office of chairman, for in 1964 Joseph Terry and Sons Limited joined the Forté Group (thus acquiring resources for continued expansion), and Lord Forté was himself chairman for a time.

Early in 1977 Terry's became part of the Colgate-Palmolive Group of Companies. Then in February 1982 they were taken over by United Biscuits UK Limited and became part of their major trading division, UB Biscuits UK Limited. As recently as 1988, prior to the acquisition of the Callard and Bowser Company, Terry's formed a separate division within United Biscuits and now trades

under the identity of the Terry's Group, a development which would surely gratify the apothecary Joseph Terry, who as a boy flattened his nose against the window of Bayldon and Berry's comfit shop in Bootham, York.

Joseph would no doubt also be impressed, if rather surprised, to find that the Terry's he founded had embarked on a new expansion campaign, as recently as 1990, to make its products 'the flavour of Europe' by acquiring the French speciality firm Chocometz SA. Thus they gained outlets in new areas including Germany and the Benelux countries. A still more recent acquisition by United Biscuits has been Verkade, a biscuit and confectionery manufacturer in Holland, with which Terry's works closely on the confectionery side.

A story of many changes, certainly. What, if any, I asked Peter, had been the constant factors? 'We always stressed to ourselves that we were the makers of quality products', he said. 'I think, in all honesty, that in that endeavour we were outstanding in this country. Possibly our main competitors in the old days would be the Swiss. But in the days when I was active, the amount of imported chocolate was less than two per cent, so they hardly came into it. Now, I understand, it has risen to almost ten per cent. Barker and Dobson in this country used to make chocolates of a comparable quality and price to Terry's. They had an assortment akin to our *All Gold* and selling at three and eightpence a half pound!' He smiled at the accuracy of his recollections.

John Earnshaw, Factory Director, commented, 'Looking back to the early thirties, when Terry's was beginning to find their real place in the market, we see them making a wide range of high quality plain chocolate. (In those days we weren't making milk chocolate.) We can also see from early brochures that Terry's products were already exceptionally well packaged and offered superb variety. There's no doubt whatever that the company raised standards in those fields.' This emphasis on quality has produced some good stories. There was for instance, Sir Francis Terry, who, when offered a tray of centres for his approval, is said to have tasted one and thrown the rest out of the window.

Terry's is the family firm par excellence, Peter N L Terry is the nephew of Sir Francis, who

*A combination of hi-tech and hands-on labour assembles Easter eggs*

*Last of the Terrys to be involved in the company, Peter Terry, as honorary life president, retains a keen interest in its progress*

was chairman for thirty-five years (1923–1958). The shop floor, too, has seen its dynasties of four or five generations. But family ties, it would seem, sometimes extended only as far as the factory gate, or in some cases the departmental door! 'Do you work in here?' enquired a father when his recently hired young son called to visit him in the boiling shops at Clementhorpe. 'No, Dad', the lad replied. 'Well, get out then', was his father's gruff injunction. In the office building there is a remarkable picture gallery extending along corridors for nearly a quarter of a mile on which are displayed photographs of the multitudes of Terry's employees who have served the company for fifty years or more. This is affectionately known as the Rogues Gallery.

The people of York are undeniably proud of Terry's, and none more so than those who have worked in this home of fine chocolates. Today, one can sense the good relationship existing between

management and workforce, but the situation was not always quite so harmonious. Keen on their work though they doubtless were, the shop-floor personnel sometimes felt they were entitled to more leisure. Hence the copperplate, carefully deferential petition (obviously not their first) presented to the management in 1853: 'Gentlemen, We the undersigned servants in your employment, in respectfully presenting to you this our earnest petition desire, first, gratefully to acknowledge the favour you have already bestowed upon us in the diminution of our hours of labour . . .'

Just over forty years later, in 1894, a round robin bearing 153 signatures invoked 'the Nine Hours movement which we consider to be beneficial to our health and in so doing we are only seeking that rest and recreation on which are enjoyed by all other trades and professions'. No doubt their pleas were heeded to the benefit of all concerned.

*Terry's factory gates at dusk. The tower is a landmark*

*Chocolate oranges being fed into the automatic foiling and pleating machine*

How those signatories would goggle if they could tour the extensive ramifications of the Terry's of today. For the company is now a remarkable example of industrial evolution. As Jeff Moss, Research and Development Controller, explained: 'We have developed what were essentially craft elements in chocolate manufacture into automated processes requiring a minimum of hands-on skill.'

'The most revolutionary example of automated production has to be the initial processing of cocoa in the liquor refinery, or "mass plant". There we take the raw cocoa and process it to the stage where it has been cleaned, shelled, roasted and made micro-biologically safe. Thus we have achieved real state-of-the-art liquor processing which other companies have followed. It was a United Biscuits intiative that we should install the liquor refinery plant at Terry's, because we produce the cocoa for them; but Terry's own requirements were also very much a part of the scheme.'

A much older process that also appears to defy automation, is the tasting of cocoa samples in the form of a paste made from roasted beans. To the untrained palate this substance might appear to be anything but appealing, yet it reveals to the taster whether or not the cocoa he is sampling has, for instance, the right 'floral' flavours (violet, maybe, or rose) required for the perfect chocolate 'bouquet' that is Terry's aim.

While in many activities, such as chocolate decoration, craftsmen may seem to have been largely replaced by technicians, when it comes to packing boxes of chocolate assortments, 'skilled packers can beat the best robots', says Jeff Moss. They can deftly turn pieces the right way to fit the box and even carry out a quality control operation as they pack by discarding any damaged items. 'You'll never get a machine to do all that as effectively at the same speed.'

We shall probably never be able to 'automate' the weather, which of course affects the cropping of the cocoa trees; and there will always be other imponderables, such as, the mysterious 'burnt rubber' taste that was at one time found to affect some Pacific-type cocoas. Eventually it was discovered that local workers had been using old tyres as fuel on the cocoa-driers.

But for all the inherited wisdom, the craft and the technology that underlie Terry's output, their efforts would be fruitless without a keen awareness of the changes in our way of life that determine customers' preferences. So whilst a box of *All Gold* still makes a very acceptable gift, it now has to compete with other attractions such as flowers or a bottle of wine.

And there are other changes: 'People tend to snack more today', says Jeff. Hence the popularity of cereal-based bars which can be put in a lunch box and Terry's tries to be responsive to such market changes. After careful research they developed *Moments* luxury chocolates aimed at young female consumers.

So what of the future? 'I feel it must be rosy', said the self-styled 'last of the Terry clan', life president Peter, 'not only in this country but abroad too, particularly in Europe, wherever quality chocolate is appreciated.' John Earnshaw agreed. As far as Terry's is concerned, he pointed out, integration with the continent is already well under way, with products flowing in both directions. 'Terry's have always had a sound export trade, but increasingly we shall be catering for a much larger market place.'

And despite all the changes, Terry's chocolates are still made in Yorkshire – the manufacturing base remains where Terry's originated, in the county capital, although so much else has changed over the years to equip the company to trade in the wider world.

# Drystone waller

## Jason of the Brontë Moors

Jason Reeve is a drystone waller by choice, and a man of independent views. He is noticeably self-sufficient; he has to be, for walling is a lonely occupation. So when Jason drives to his jobs in his big-wheeled red pick-up, affectionately referred to as 'the beast', he is also accompanied by Sally, his vocal and energetic Jack Russell. Jason lives at Moorlodge Farm, Oakworth, near Haworth on the Brontë moors. He finds it hard to say exactly when (without benefit of cement), he first laid stone on stone and saw what he had built resist wind and weather. Now he can point with pride to many memorials to his craftsmanship, but he is even more than a craftsman – he is a champion.

So how did he begin? 'With living on a farm', he says, 'I often had to mend gaps in the walls. I'd be around ten year old then.' He learned his first tricks of the trade from his step-father, tenant of Moorlodge Farm – 'and then I sort o' picked it up myself.' Just how does a waller 'pick it up'? Did he learn from books, for instance, studying the various styles found in different parts of Yorkshire's moors and dales? 'I have a few books at home', he said. 'I've read through 'em, but mostly I've learned by practice.'

Jason is young and strong, as he needs to be. I have met a stone waller in his sixties, but such veterans are not very numerous, for working outdoors on the bleak northern uplands reveals weaknesses in physique as surely as frost seeks out cracks in stone. It probably proves the seriousness of Jason's intentions that by the time he was thirteen he had already obtained a walling tent, made to his own specifications, 21 feet long, 14 feet wide and 6 feet 6 inches high, so that he was less vulnerable to the weather. 'I've walled under there while it's been snowing outside,' he said, 'with a little coal fire in a bucket. But if it gets that bad I'd sooner be sitting by a fire at home!'

He first joined the elite of his craft when he was about fourteen, competing in a junior class in one

*A young Jason readily tackles a gap in a wall*

of the most famous of Wharfedale agricultural shows – Kilnsey Show – with the upper age limit set at twenty-one. And having won it once, he went on to win it 'one or two more times', as he tells you laconically. Since then he has competed annually and his tally of local wins includes three at Pateley Bridge Show, two at Horton-in-Ribblesdale, plus another one or two at Malham. Almost as an afterthought he adds that he has been British champion twice – the first time when he was nineteen and competing against perhaps seventy other entrants – and he has taken second place 'by a point or two' when the event has been held in Scotland.

How does one set about competing to become a walling champ? It starts with a ballot in the morning. Then each contestant, having picked a number out, finds the five-foot-high, three-yard-long stretch of wall he's won in the draw and proceeds to pull it down. 'You take your top stones off and you put 'em well back in a line so you don't mess 'em up,' explains Jason. 'You put your little ones back as well, sorting all your stones out as you go. And once you've got your wall down, you put your footings in – your foundations, that is – with your bigger stones, you set them about four or five inch down after taking the sod off. Your wall is about twenty-six to thirty inches wide at the bottom; you have two sides and in the middle you put all your fillings, and keep it going level all the way up. You have to course it through – you'll never win anything with random walling. So you make sure you cross all your joints so that there's no straight joints as you go up the wall. See?' Well, more or less, if what Jason meant was that you aimed for the alternating, eye-pleasing symmetry achieved in brickwork. Which prompts the thought that the first aesthetes were probably not precious young men starving in garrets, but sons of toil with tools in their hands and the fabric of the earth for their material.

'Then, when you get to two foot high, you put your through-stones in to hold it all together.' The through-stones, inserted at every two feet in height and every yard in 'running length', are inclined to vary from one locality to another. Sometimes they

*Drystone waller Jason Reeve has two companions in what can be at times a lonely life – his pick-up and his Jack Russell, Sally*

*Inset: Jason, twice British champion, is seen here working on a Worth Valley farm in his early teens*

*Not many craftsmen use as few tools as the waller. His chief aid is an eye for just the stone he needs; but occasionally a hammer comes in handy*

protrude from both sides of the wall, but sometimes from only one. 'Traditionally', says Jason, 'the through-stones protrude on the side of the owner of the field'.

Wallers compete in a number of classes, starting with beginners, who might be as young as nine. There are also classes for amateur and professional 'singles' and 'pairs', as well as 'mastercraft' classes. Pairs, with a six-yard stretch of wall to build, work one at each side of it. Jason never competes as one of a pair: 'I just like to be on my own.' It's a pleasant, if surprising, fact that competitive walling seems to be increasing in popularity. 'Every year you seem to see more wallers at the shows', he says.

In competitions the stone you 'draw' can be a vital factor. 'You can have a rough load and you're jiggered for the day, but if you're a good waller and you've drawn a good lot, you've a fair chance.' He finds it easier to work with the sort of stone he knows, but considers that the comparatively generous time allowed for competitive work offsets any disadvantage of unfamiliar stone. Although his experience now covers a wide variety, in his native moorlands his material is mostly dour-looking sandstone; in the

Dales he handles the silvery limestone. And the stones he uses to reassemble the walls he has just demolished may have been used for hundreds of years, passing through the hands of long-dead wallers.

Competition practices vary: 'Up Scotland, you double-wall to three foot high, as we do here, and course it through. Then, to bring it up to four foot six' (the regulation height), 'you do it in single walling, an' that's a bit more of a struggle. The first time I did it up there, I'd never done that single-walling to the top before, but I came second all the same. So I didn't do too bad.' A modest enough assessment when you consider that making one stone stand up is probably at least twice as difficult as achieving the trick with two – especially to a height of eighteen inches.

Is there a secret knack which must be acquired before a waller can hope to succeed in competitions, where speed is necessary to avoid 'struggling' as finishing time looms closer? According to Jason, you either have walling 'in you' or you don't. The judgement to recognise at first sight the stone you need just when you want it is essential, but practice helps too. 'I used to pick up stone after stone, but now I seem to go straight to the one I want.'

In addition to competing, Jason has demonstrated his craft at shows at Bolton Abbey and Otley, and at the Broughton Game Fair. At Harewood House, Lord Harewood was so impressed with one of Jason's demonstration walls that he asked for it to be left standing, even though it was in the middle of a field!

Walling can be heavy work, but Jason makes light of difficulties. Asked what is the hardest thing he has to tackle, he thinks for fully five seconds before answering. Then, 'Walling up a hillside', he says, 'because you've got to go level with your courses into the bank.' I can think of few other sentences that more succinctly describe the waller's problems with gravity.

His most interesting job of all, he says, was at the Hampton Court Flower Show and it came his way via the Drystone Walling Association, of which he is a member. About forty different gardens had been specially created as exhibits and Jason had to surround one of them with thirty metres of drystone walling, two feet high. This was to be surmounted by – of all things – a miniature railway. If any chance of a mini-disaster was to be avoided, the wall had to provide a perfectly level base for the track, yet Jason and an assistant performed their task in two days, working till half-past ten at night, starting next morning at five-thirty and working through till 11pm. He found the Southerners quite fascinated by the unfamiliar sight of walls being built without cement.

But why build them that way? Wouldn't a cement-bound wall be stronger? It would certainly be more expensive. Consider the cost in money, time and effort of carting loads of sand and cement about precipitously sloping Pennine fields. On the open hills, where temperatures are continually changing, cement would eventually crumble, whereas a good drystone wall allows room for expansion and contraction. Its open construction admits the wind to dry it, and should a blundering cow or tractor knock it down, the stones are still there to be reassembled. A well-built drystone wall, says Jason, will last a lifetime, marking boundaries and giving shelter to man and beast. With pride he tells you that the drystone 'den' he built when he was nine stands as firmly as ever today.

Jason is occasionally asked to run courses for would-be wallers who might be anything from young offenders to retired police chiefs. But he is happiest when following his craft alone, preferably building a garden wall for a customer who appreciates a handsome job. However, due to the rate at which his business is developing, he might soon have to become an employer in spite of himself: 'I've already got work for twelve months ahead', he says.

At twenty-three, he has some shrewd ideas about his future. 'With the weather we get up here, my bones ache even now', he grins. He might carry on walling until he's forty, he thinks, then occupy himself renovating property – preferably stone-built. 'Doing-up' old cottages, he's sure, would suit him down to the ground – or should I say up to the roof?

*Laying courses on a new gritstone wall calls for careful selection of stones*

# The York Glaziers' Trust

*And storied windows richly dight,*
*Casting a dim religious light.*
*There let the pealing organ blow,*
*To the full-voiced quire below.*

John Milton

When Peter Gibson was five years old he went missing from his home in Precentor's Court in the shadow – no mere cliché – of York Minster. The house, in which he still lives today, was searched but revealed no trace of him. He had, he says, apparently vanished from the face of the earth. Fortunately for his mother's peace of mind, it was not long before one of the Minster's own policemen walked the short distance from York's Metropolitan Church of St Peter to Precentor's Court to tell her: 'Your Peter's sitting on the steps of the high altar in his pyjamas'.

It might appear fanciful to cite this event as the start of one man's love affair with a cathedral, and yet it could be argued that had Peter ever married, his wife might well have seen the Minster as her most formidable rival. In different circumstances Peter Gibson might have become a priest. He makes a point of explaining that his work as Superintendent of the York Glaziers' Trust is an expression of his faith, linking him with the medieval craftsman who would lavish loving artistry on a tiny detail in the Minster roof though it were visible 'only to the eye of God'.

A few years after the Minster escapade, young Peter became a chorister at the church where Guy Fawkes was christened, St Michael-le-Belfrey, 'next door' to the beloved Minster. By the time he was thirteen he had become a Minster altar server, whose obvious interest in church matters attracted the notice of the then Dean of York, Dr Eric Milner-White. The acquaintance deepened when Dr Milner-White went to Nunthorpe Secondary

School, which Peter attended, to present the prizes on Speech Day. The Dean was an expert on the Minster's glass and other treasures and soon after the visit Peter was given a grand tour of the glass workshop, and invited to browse in the Deanery library, from where he went home burdened with three books on stained glass. At the Dean's suggestion, he 'tried the work out' in the workshop. He has been 'trying it out', he says, 'ever since.' Now he is not only Secretary and Superintendent of the York Glaziers' Trust but an international authority on stained glass.

He has travelled over half a million miles to lecture in churches, prisons, schools, cathedrals, on radio and on TV. He was awarded the MBE in 1984 and has a cluster of honorary degrees, fellowships and other honours bestowed in Britain, Italy and the USA. Yet today he never enters York Minster without glancing towards the restored Great East Window some seventy feet above the ground ('the finest fifteenth century window in the world') which contains a number of herringbone panels in red and purple glass. No more than twelve inches high, they are incomparably special to him since they represent his own apprentice contribution to the re-leading of a masterpiece.

If ever a man grew in harness with his job it is Peter Gibson. He has responsibilities for stained glass conservation far beyond the medieval walls of his native city, which, as he delights to tell you, is one of the greatest stained glass centres in the world. The Minster alone contains the largest accumulated collection of medieval stained glass in England – 128 windows representing every period of glass painting from the twelfth century to the present day – 'in other words, a complete visual commentary on the art and craft of glass painting spanning eight hundred years'.

He is committed to lectures as far ahead as he can see. 'I've just come back from the States after lecturing in the National Cathedral in Washington, which has about two hundred windows. Six centuries from now, I hope and pray, people will hold

*Mark Bamborough at work on the conservation of fourteenth century glass from a north nave aisle window of York Minster*

Washington Cathedral in as much regard as we now hold York Minster, as a great treasure house of stained glass. Though it's modern glass now, it too will be old some day, but only if it is properly cared for, as I'm sure it will be'.

When that time comes, six centuries hence, the oldest glass in England – from St Paul's Church, Jarrow – will be approaching the second millennium of its age, for it was made in the seventh or eighth century AD. It was restored in the Glaziers' Trust workshop under Peter Gibson's direction, but it bears no signature, either of artist or restorer. 'When I lecture', he said, 'I'm often asked if I sign the windows I work on. I never would, not in a thousand years, if it were left to me. On two occasions I was powerless to prevent it, but you'll not see my name on any Minster window nor should it be there. All I'm doing is ensuring that the work done by craftsmen centuries ago lives on for future generations. The people who deserve the credit and their names on the glass are the men who created those windows four, five, six hundred years ago.'

Only Chartres Cathedral can rank with York Minster for its wealth of glass, though the glass in that great French church is mainly twelfth or early thirteenth century in date and therefore lacks the wonderful catholicity to be found in York. But even if there were no stained glass at all in the Minster, which contains two million separate pieces in all, the gorgeous treasury that is spread through the city's parish churches would be enough in itself to make York a world centre of glass painting.

Conceivably, Hitler's 'Baedeker' air raids (strange weapons for a supposed artist) could have destroyed this heritage had it not been for the foresight of the authorities of the time. As it was, a

*Above: Superintendent Peter Gibson examines a fifteenth century head in the Trust workshop's glass 'bank'*

*Right: Minster from glaziers' workshop*

Above: Bryony Benwell waterproofing a panel. Unlike the craftsmen seen in other pictures, Bryony is still serving her apprenticeship

Left: Guildhall and River Ouse from Lendal Bridge

raid in April 1942 destroyed York's historic Guildhall and St Martin's Church, but the greatest of the Minster windows were already safe. For in 1939 eighty of them had been removed and stored far from the light of day in the cellars of some of Yorkshire's great houses, or buried beneath the bar walls of the city.

With peace came the task of reassembling what the press called 'the largest jigsaw puzzle in the world'. Under the guidance of Eric Milner-White, three Minster glaziers, including Peter Gibson, attempted, in his words, 'to recreate the original stories told by the Minster windows'. Window by window, the Minster's glazed glory was restored at great financial cost, much of it borne by one of the city's chief benefactors, the Pilgrim Trust. Probably about this time was born the hope that in years to come York would be a centre of stained glass restoration that would not only benefit the Minster and York's historic parish churches but would be a focus of stained glass restoration and conservation for the whole of Britain.

Thus it was that on 1 September 1967 the York Glaziers' Trust came into being, the Pilgrim Trust having already given a grant of about £6,000 for the

modernising and re-equipment of the old Dean and Chapter workshop; Peter Gibson justly describes his vocation as 'the undying craft'; its basic principles have hardly changed since the Middle Ages, but even the ancient craft of stained glass work can benefit from twentieth century technology. One example of this is the 'ultra-sonic bath', which applies science to the extremely delicate task of cleaning ancient panes and panels, sometimes literally wafer-thin due to weathering. Paradoxically, this is not simply a matter of cleaning the glass. 'You could even make it look too clean by over-cleaning', he explains: 'Or you could use the wrong product.' Hence the ultra-sonic bath, in which glass placed in stainless steel baskets is immersed in dilute ammonia through which ultra-sonic vibrations are transmitted by means of a generator. The dirt is shaken away but the finest painted detail remains undamaged. During the formidable post-war restoration of the Minster glass, the tiny team of three glaziers had no such aids, not even the fibreglass brushes used today. It was simply a matter of soft cloths, the minimum use of water and infinite care.

Such innovations apart, the basic technique of making 'stained and painted glass' (to use the full and accurate term) has changed surprisingly little over the years. As he explained in a necessarily brief outline: 'Glass is stained various colours in the course of manufacture by mixing in metallic oxides while it is in its molten state. If you want blue you put cobalt in the molten glass. If you want red glass you use oxide of copper, and so on. Then the glass comes to the workshops in sheets, just as it did in the Middle Ages. It is cut to shape and the details are painted and fired on to the surface.' The pieces of glass are held together by H-shaped sections of lead. Being flexible and durable, as well as easily cut and soldered, lead is ideal for the job. Then finally comes the waterproofing.

Past centuries as well as modern science lend their aid to restoration, as Peter's prized 'glass bank' demonstrates. With its seven thousand invaluable pieces covering eight hundred years of the glass painter's craft, it can furnish on demand an angel, a bishop or the haloed head of a saint. What is the most difficult task in a job fraught with problems? 'If, as frequently happens, we get panels in that are

in a very misordered state – veritable jigsaws – our most difficult task is to sort out the glass, and, if we have licence and authority to attempt any rearrangement, do just that', he said.

Trusteeship of the York Glaziers' Trust is shared between the Pilgrim Trust and the Dean and Chapter of York, under the chairmanship of the present Dean, the Very Reverend Dr John Southgate. Rooted strongly though it is in York, the Trust's customers may come almost literally 'from anywhere'. Since it was formed, something like a thousand commissions have been completed in cathedrals, parish churches, great houses and museums up and down the land, and all this is in addition to the endless activities involving the Minster.

'We've been working for the past three years on the fourteenth century glass at the Chapter House at Wells Cathedral', says Peter Gibson. 'In the workshop we have glass from New College Chapel, Oxford, part of the most important collection of late fourteenth century glass in England. And we've recently completed work on six windows at the eastern end of the apse of Peterborough Cathedral. Some months ago, we completed work on the west window of the Parish Church at Berwick-on-Tweed, where there is a lovely and very important collection of sixteenth and seventeenth century roundels. It doesn't matter whether it's a great collection of thousands of panels of stained glass or just one panel, this workshop exists to restore that glass. If some little parish church has just one piece of medieval glass, to that church it is just as priceless a treasure as York's great collection is to the Dean and Chapter.'

But Peter's work involves him with more than medieval glass. Some forty years ago, when St Paul's Church, Middlesborough, was about to be demolished, he and a colleague set out to rescue the early twentieth century glass in the East window, some of which found a home in the Minster. Another of his responsibilities is the care of the second largest collection in the world of Swiss-stained glass: it was removed from Wragby parish church in the grounds of Nostell Priory, near Wakefield, because of possible danger from mining subsidence, and is due to be reinstated when conditions allow.

However, the conservation of York Minster's medieval glass alone is an endless task. Recent years have seen the completion of work on the Great West

*Rodney Beaumont puts together the outer-protective glass*

Window, which had to be taken out six or seven years ago because the stonework needed renewal. When the ancient glass was re-inserted new external protective glazing was installed, cut to the design and shape of the medieval glass. In other words, a second Great West Window was made in clear glass, so that when you look at the window from inside, you're unaware of the protective glazing, because it follows the same leadwork design of the medieval glass. When you go outside and look at the West window, the leadwork pattern of the protective glass is far more aesthetically acceptable than simply diamond-shaped pieces of glass, which was the case with the old method.

On 9 July 1984 lightning (the most probable cause) almost succeeded, where Hitler's bombers had failed, in destroying York Minster. What Peter Gibson's state of mind must have been the morning after that catastrophe it is impossible to imagine. From a vantage point eighty feet above the ground, at some risk to life and limb, he took what he believes was a unique photograph of the gorgeous Rose Window, stark against the ruined Minster roof and the sky. The Rose Window's restoration, says Peter Gibson, was the most important work to have gone through his hands. Its sixteenth century glass, cracked by the heat into 40,000 fragments, had to be removed, secured together with an adhesive, sandwiched between two layers of plain glass and replaced. That is quickly said, but it meant two years' work for the workshop. 'That piece of restoration captured the imagination of people all over the world', says Peter Gibson.

On 4 November 1988 the Queen attended a service of thanksgiving for the restoration of the Minster. Later, visiting the Glaziers' Trust workshops, Her Majesty was shown how the Rose Window had been restored. 'Now', says Gibson, 'we hope and pray that it's good for another five hundred years.'

The workshop of the York Glaziers' Trust has the peaceful atmosphere found only where men are working at a craft they love. The workshop team consists of six craftsmen, an assistant to the Superintendent (Peter) and the workshop's first female apprentice, who, at the age of twenty-four, is engaged on a four-year novitiate, having come to the workshop with some knowledge of stained glass already gained from previous studies.

Peter's own apprenticeship lasted seven years,

then the traditionally accepted term in many crafts. He feels this should still be the norm, but in this workshop, even more important than length of tutelage or technical qualifications (essential though they are), must be keenness to work on medieval-glass conservation together with a 'sympathy' for the glass, in all its fragility: 'Sometimes it's literally wafer-thin.'

Craftsmen joining the studio from 'commercial' concerns, where they have learned the 'basics' of glazing, find they've entered 'a new world and must start to learn a new job'. But those who master this demanding 'living craft' need hardly fear unemployment, thanks not only to Britain's wealth of medieval glass but to the Gothic Revival in the second half of the nineteenth century, during which thousands of churches were built in Britain.

The life of a stained glass window (which is essentially, that of its lead), is about a hundred years, 'so coming up in the next twenty to thirty years', Peter explains, 'there are going to be hundreds, if not thousands, of stained glass windows requiring the attention of skilled craftsmen'. It really is a living craft! A hundred years from now, people will still be judging the work done in stained glass today and in past centuries.

What of the centuries to come? 'The craft is undergoing a great revival of interest', he says, 'both here and abroad. There are in this country hundreds of glass painters, whereas when I began my apprenticeship, entry into the craft was not so fashionable. You can now go on a degree course in architectural glass, and if students coming out of college can't find a job in a workshop they'll set up their own, so there are lots of new workshops developing.

'Even without York, even without the Minster,' says Peter Gibson, 'there is no craft associated with Yorkshire that is more important than stained glass.' A remarkable claim, yet who better qualified than he to make it? There are certainly few crafts more ancient, and few, it would seem, whose future prospects might even surpass their illustrious past.

*The time-honoured skills of leading and soldering are used on new pieces produced to protect the old*

# Clever clogs
## – and clogmakers at Hebden Bridge

*Clogs are cool in summer's heat*
*Clogs are warm in winter's sleet*

On the wall of Walkley Clogs at Hebden Bridge is a wealth of advertising (c. 1929) extolling the virtues of clogs. 'You must keep his feet warm', warns a solemn-faced doctor to the mother of the small boy he is examining: 'I advise clogs.' Another ad shows a happy millgirl wearing not only a long tartan shawl but its traditional corollary, a pair of clogs. She, the headline proudly declares, is one of 'The Nation's Clogwearers'.

But these are only moderate expressions of enthusiasm for what the French call sabots; for another advertisement suggests that you can even go to sea in this footwear 'for all conditions'. A couple of jolly kiddiwinkies are shown hoisting their sail and doing just that. But why, if clogs are so good for you, did the makers need to go to such lengths to advertise them? When I went to school, clogs were worn by kids who were very good at fighting with them and kicking sparks out of the pavement but whose parents were hardly considered well off. Perhaps clogs were going downmarket in the twenties and the makers were doing their best to reverse the trend.

If so they seem to have succeeded – or somebody has. Walk into Walkley's on any day in the 1990s except Christmas Day and Boxing Day and you gain the distinct impression that people love clogs. Otherwise, why should 250,000 people visit the works each year by all kinds of transport including horse-drawn barges which stop at the Walkley works on summer trips along the Rochdale Canal. Clogs have always had their fans, of course. Mark Clynde's mother wore them at school in Nottinghamshire – not that she'd any interest in fighting with them: she was, after all, the teacher.

Mark is managing director of Walkley Clogs, housed in a towering building at Hebden Bridge which has been used in clog manufacture since it was built in 1851. His interest may stem partly from

*Nelson Rush reaches for a piece of welting*

the fact that both his grandfather, a barrel-maker, and his mother wore clogs – hers were bought from a maker in Barnsley and later at Hebden Bridge. At one time only the soles were made in Hebden, by Maude's Clog Soles, who supplied all the clog-makers in the United Kingdom. However, the whole product has been manufactured there since 1973, when Walkley's, a firm of clog-makers then based in Huddersfield, decided to buy the Hebden Bridge factory to preserve their own supply of soles.

Suddenly in the mid-seventies there came a big steel strike and this, says Mark, along with the exploitation of natural gas, caused most of Walkley's market for clogs to disappear virtually overnight. For at a time when every town of any size had its own gas works, and a man toiling on the slag heaps could go through a pair of clogs in an hour, Walkley's biggest customer of all had been the nation-wide gas industry.

In order to rationalise the company, Walkley's disposed of the Huddersfield premises and centred

*Above: John Merrick sawing beech blocks for clogmaking*

*Left: brothers Nelson (left) and Gordon Rush*

their entire undertaking on Hebden Bridge. Today this enterprise claims to be 'the only surviving clog mill where skills have been passed on over the decades'.

At Hebden Bridge (which styles itself 'The Pennine Centre') Walkley's make over 25,000 pairs of clogs a year – clogs for agriculture and industry, clogs to feature, they say, in the collections of top couturiers in places as footwear-conscious as Italy. 'About half our clogs are sold either into the alternative fashion market or to visitors to the mill.' The latter products are very much the traditional Yorkshire or Lancashire clogs. Not touristy imitations, says Mark, but 'the real McCoy'. Inevitably there have been changes in the industry. 'I suppose the main difference is that while we still make clogs with the traditional irons on the sole, the bulk of our production has either an imitation-iron horseshoe-shaped rubber, or the sort of rubber soles that you might get on mountain boots. They still have the wooden sole of course.'

British Steel and most of its subsidiaries still absorb the bulk of the Walkley output of industrial clogs. The rest goes into other branches of heavy

engineering – Ford, ICI, British Coal and even something as modern as British Nuclear Fuels. What mysterious virtues, I wondered, made this apparently antiquated footwear so irreplaceable? Mark explained: clogs will survive in any environment where there are extremes of heat, wet or a combination of the two. The wood sole is a superb natural insulator, the leather – thicker than used in the average boot – also affords great protection to the wearer. 'We have steel-workers in Cleveland who effectively are walking in molten steel, where no boot would come anywhere near giving protection.'

The wood used for clog soles was traditionally alder, but because the clog industry made such

*Top left: John Merrick operating the side-cutter, another process in clogmaking*

*Left: fixing a sole to a clog*

*Above: Gordon Rush trims the rubber sole and demonstrates the use of a clogmaker's tool of bygone days, the stock knife*

inroads into alder forests, beech is now used instead. (At one time, beech itself was under threat due to the continuing demand from the clogmakers.) The leather used in industrial clogs comes either from cows or from Indian buffalo. The uppers of non-industrial clogs, however, are made from traditional British hide.

Standing idle today near the entrance to Walkley's works is an implement called a stock knife. It has a blade rather like that of a scythe, and a handle which clogmakers of many decades ago would wield with almost unbelievable skill and speed to produce the countless clog soles needed by the labouring masses.

Gordon Rush, who like his brother Nelson has been a clogmaker for many years, looks back with admiration and some sympathy to his predecessors who had to labour long and hard with this rather ferocious-looking tool. The methods employed today are not only quicker and faster, they are certainly easier on the operatives' physiques.

The beech planks which are stacked to season outside the works are first cut to the size of the sole required, then denuded of their corners before being fixed to the 'copping lathe' which, guided by a template, turns them to the required size and shape. The leather uppers are hammered on with remarkable speed and dexterity by a man using long, large-headed nails which bite deep into the close-grained beech. Still very much in use are the clogmaker's traditional hammer and pincers and the last, on which the clog is placed while he works on it.

On shelves just across the room were clogs in wide variety, including elegant 'Sunday clogs' adorned with a white 'snowflake pattern' of intricately arranged studs. Gordon will gladly measure you for a pair made for your personal requirements. Clogs, he claims, are such versatile articles that folk with disabilities are more easily catered for by the clog-maker than by the conventional shoemaker. Indeed, answering the problem of the handicapped is one of the great satisfactions of his craft. A small boy, who had been born without fingers and was therefore unable to lace-up ordinary shoes, was provided – to his great delight – with a pair of specially made

clogs with an easily managed patent fastener.

In December 1990 Walkley's premises was severely damaged by fire. If you can imagine a phoenix with clogs on, it would make a good symbol for the way the company has wrested ever-increasing success from apparent disaster. A £1 million refurbishment has fully restored the mill making it one of the county's leading tourist attractions.

Mark Clynde's ambition is to develop the clog market to its fullest extent. 'We've exported clogs in small quantities, both as a fashion item to Holland, traditional home of the clog, and in the industrial variety, not only to the Continent, where there are still indigenous clogmakers similar to ourselves making clogs for industry, but to a Saudi Arabian steelworks. In its time this Hebden Bridge factory was producing perhaps a million clogs a year and there were six other factories in the same group.'

Walkley's, in fact, are heirs to a great tradition. 'Wherever the map was coloured red we were sending clogs. It was a huge operation in the days of the Empire, an enormous industry. Now it has shrunk back to its craft origins. Only a small part of the building is devoted to clogmaking. In the old

*Above: the Rochdale Canal at Hebden Bridge*

*Far left: visitors in the clog shop*

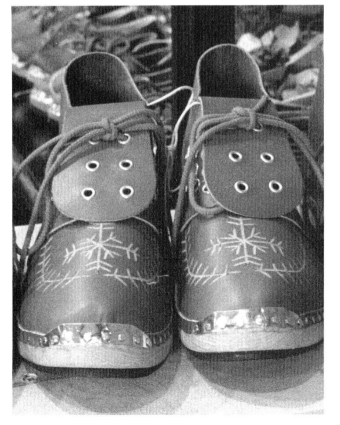

days, when it was a floor higher, the whole place was turning them out. And although this was the headquarters of the firm, it was nevertheless the smallest mill in the group.

There's a happy, family feeling at Walkley's today. I remarked on it to Mark as we sat in the restaurant with its beech furniture matching the soles of the clogs. He explained: 'We work hard at making it a nice place to visit, and when you're trying hard to cater for people, they respond in kind. After all, there aren't many places where you can just walk in without charge and wander round.'

There's certainly plenty to see, for the old clog mill has become a centre for a number of specialist crafts and retail outlets. And it's good to know that there is still a use for such historic footwear. As I said goodbye to clog-maker Gordon Rush that chilly November morning, he told me, 'I think I'll put my clogs on now – my feet are getting cold!'

# A jolly good book whereon to look . . .

## is better to me than gold

In the Wharfedale town of Otley, birthplace of that classic printing workhorse, the Wharfedale printing press, you will find the renowned printers and bookbinders, Smith Settle. Ken Smith and Brian Settle first met while working together, at nearby Ilkley, for the Scolar Press. They decided to pool their expertise and love of books and in 1981 launched their own business in what used to be a large worsted mill on the old Ilkley road. It is still spacious enough to be shared by a variety of enterprises, but fortunately there is still ample elbow room for a craft that demands more space than most.

In many ways the two men complement each other. Ken is as unmistakably Yorkshire as Brian is clearly Lancastrian. Both suffer interviews patiently but you get the impression that if they were less courteous they could give you quite a list of things they would rather do. Brian was destined to be a letterpress printer, but had to change course, because, he says, 'They said I was colour blind'. Now he is glad things turned out as they did, because he much prefers the variety and challenge of book-binding to 'just standing and watching a machine'.

Like Ken he is a voracious reader, but admits in his humorously lugubrious way to having 'book-binder's disease' – 'Every time I pick up a book, I look first of all to see where it was bound and printed and then for any faults that might be in it. And if there is anything wrong I find it!' Such fatalism might well be endemic in craftsmen of every kind. He finds the progress made by Smith Settle in the past ten years almost incredible. Much of their success he attributes to the accessibility of the two principals, plus a determined adherence to delivery dates.

'Making books is a skilled trade', Jean de la Bruyère said, sometime in the seventeenth century, 'like making clocks.' He was probably thinking of writing books rather than binding them. But whether you're writing or binding, this admittedly skilled task hardly resembles making clocks. Or does it? Having persuaded Ken Smith to talk about his beloved craft, you realise that a book at least resembles a clock in that it is a piece of engineering, and one required to withstand much rougher handling than most other artefacts. Even so, the materials that usually go into its construction are rarely stronger than paper, cardboard, cloth, thread and glue.

Ken Smith finds it difficult to decide what awakened his passion for 'the printed word', a phrase often on his lips. Without doubt a potent factor was his ability to read at the age of four. He was born in the old mill town of Batley, within walking distance of Stringer's, the second-hand book dealers of Dewsbury, who knew him well. Having laid out all his pocket money on their offerings he would spend the whole week reading, turning up at Stringer's the following Saturday to 'return the empties' and use the refund to subsidise his next literary 'fix'.

If he had not fallen so hopelessly in love with books, you feel, he might have become a detective! From Enid Blyton's Famous five he graduated to Agatha Christie via Wilkie Collins, who wrote *The Moonstone*, widely acknowledged to be 'the first English detective story'. The choice of reading seems significant when he adds that it was the construction of the stories that attracted him to these writers. For Ken Smith, it seems, a 'well-made book' can mean at least two things.

He gives no indication that he was ever tempted by the writing game. The reason may simply be his native Yorkshire caution – or common sense! It seems as likely, though, that his strong artistic streak finds expression in designing books while leaving him free to read purely for pleasure. That certainly sounds like having the best of two worlds. His father died young, a fact which probably resulted in Ken's generally serious demeanour. He knew he had to make his contribution to the family fortunes and never seems to have doubted that his future lay in the printing industry. There was little doubt, either, that of all the varied options open to a young entrant – litho artist, compositor, binder – he chose

wisely: 'I have absolutely no regrets at all that I decided on binding', he says. Of all printing activities, he believes binding is probably one of the least affected by technology. Technology may have speeded up production, but the basic process is essentially the same.

How old is the craft that can awaken such dedication? Binding in fact pre-dates printing by moveable type, which was introduced to England by Caxton in the fifteenth century. In a sense, even the monkish writings known as the incunabula were 'bound', in that the hand-written sheets were all held together by thongs or laced into boards, and the famous *Codex Sinaiticus*, a fourth century Greek manuscript version of the Bible, was held together by some method. In a sense, even the early scrolls were 'bound' since binding is basically a method of preserving the written or printed sheets.

The more you learn about bookbinding, the more you wonder whether it is an art or a craft. The basic requirement, as with any craft, is an interest in the

*Otley – the view up Kirkgate towards the Chevin*

*Ken Smith (standing) and Brian Settle with their biggest book, a monogram on the rhinoceros*

end product which, with experience, becomes a practised skill. In bookbinding especially, believes Ken Smith, you have to enjoy working with your hands, you need to be exceptionally clean and tidy and have an eye for detail and therefore a feeling for design. But in creating its best examples the craft surely becomes an art – reflected in the sensitivity with which the binding is married to the book the author wrote, in which paper, typography and covering match the character and quality of the book itself. It is an aim which becomes more difficult to achieve as standardisation of papers, cloths and leathers increases.

Bookbinding is by no means a dying craft. There are many individual binders making a living and no doubt finding creative satisfaction producing one superb volume at a time. 'We at Smith Settle, on the other hand,' says Ken Smith, 'are a binding company, able to produce a whole edition of fine bindings.'

There are, of course, bindings and bindings. The three main styles are, 'publishers' edition' bindings, the common or garden hardback, produced maybe in thousands of copies and employing all the sophisticated methods required by high-speed mass production. Then there are library bindings, a term which describes the treatment given to a book for which a long life is envisaged. At the very pinnacle of the binder's art is the style known as extra letterpress. Here are really sumptuous bindings where the design element plays as great a part as the actual construction of the book, with all the glory of full leather binding, gilt-edged pages and gold tooled titling.

A prime example is *The Rubaiyat of Omar Khayyám* bound by Sangorski and Sutcliffe, which incorporated 1,050 jewels, as well as inlays of silver and fine woods. This masterpiece, decorated with a peacock design, now lies at the bottom of the Atlantic having gone down with the *Titanic* when she struck an iceberg en route to the USA in 1912. A later copy was destroyed during the second world war. It is almost impossible to calculate the value of such a book today, although not long ago Sangorski and Sutcliffe's binding of Coleridge's *The Ancient Mariner* was valued at £80,000.

For all his admiration of the designer book binder's artistry, Ken Smith insists: 'I believe a book is designed to be read, rather than treated as a piece of sculpture. A binding should first and foremost be

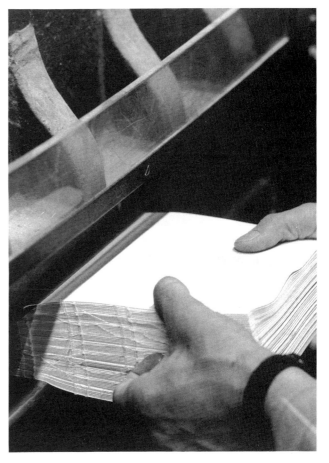

*The book blocks are nipped in this machine to remove air trapped inside the signatures during the folding and sewing stages*

serviceable in protecting and adorning the text. Smith Settle's aim is to produce well-bound books'.

That process involves various stages. From the printing machine comes a sheet of paper, printed on both sides. This has to be folded so that the pages fall into the required order.

The folded sheets are 'gathered' into sections of sixteen, twenty-four or thirty-two pages, according to the size and arrangement of the final book. The sections, also known as 'signatures', are combined in the right sequence to make what is known as a book 'block' – a complete book lacking only its cover. The cover is then attached.

The traditional craftsman bookbinder would employ a 'sewing frame' for this process, sewing the sheets around cords which would then be used to 'lace in' the boards so that they become an integral part of the book. Running down the inside and outside of each section is a length of thread, which is laced on to the adjoining 'gatherings' or sections, by what Ken Smith calls a continuous 'braiding'

motion – 'at the bottom and top of each gathering is a slip-stitch, which is looped into the previous stitch. And there you have the gatherings sewn together, and the very start of the book.'

After that, the spine is treated with adhesive to afford it some degree of flexibility during the further binding processes, and to hold the sections together. 'Otherwise, when you opened the book, the spine would gape down the back where the sections were not joined.'

Next, by means of a three-bladed 'guillotine', the bound sections are trimmed at 'top', 'tail' and 'foredge' [the front or outer edge of the pages] to a uniform size, except in the occasional cases where the edges are left uncut, known in the business as 'rough' edges.

'Rounding and backing' is the next process, during which the foredge is made concave so that the book can maintain a fairly uniform shape. A book lacking that rounded back is described as 'square-backed'. Such books because of the tension of the

sewing and repeated opening and closing of it, will eventually assume a convex shape, the sheets 'bellying out' from the middle. Rounding and backing helps to hold the book in a pleasing and uniform shape.

A survival from the craft as it was practised two or three centuries ago is the 'headband', now little more than an ornamentation. These small ribbon tapes attached to the head and tail of the spine once served to protect the leather as the book was taken from the shelf and replaced, and gave added strength to the binding. The most vulnerable part of a hardbacked book is the 'joint', the point at which the book opens, immediately between the spine and the boards. It is seen as a small groove, which acts as a hinge. With use, this tends to weaken, so it is reinforced with a strip of calico or crêpe paper.

In the case of 'publishers' edition' bindings, the book blocks are prepared separately from the hard outer cover, the case, which is made up of two pieces of board, a piece of spine 'hollow', cut to the width

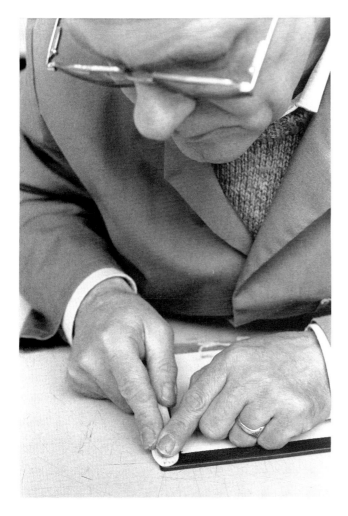

of the curvature of the spine and a piece of covering material. The case is so constructed that it wraps around the book and extends above and below the pages by approximately an eighth of an inch. The purpose of this, known as 'the square', is to keep the edges of the pages from rubbing on the shelf. The cloth is turned in and overlaid on to the inside of the boards so that, to all appearances, in the finished book the bare board is invisible, its limits being hidden, except for a slight ridge, by the end-papers.

Next the title and author's name are added in gold or some other colour on the spine or front cover. The case is then brought together with the book block by a process known as 'casing-in', which means that paste is applied to the front and back end-papers, which are positioned inside the case and brought together under pressure to secure sufficient adhesion between the end papers and the inner sides

*Far left: space is a primary requirement*

*Left and above: bookbinding is a 'hands-on' craft. Brian Settle at work*

of the boards.

In the case of letterpress binding, the boards are actually laced on to the book, of which they are an integral part. Here, says Ken Smith, the book is 'constructed, rather than made' and each book is covered individually and generally treated as a separate unit. Covering material is usually leather, which is used in several styles, named according to the extent to which leather is used. For instance, quarter binding is simply a strip of leather attached to the spine and extending perhaps a quarter of the width of the book on to the front and back boards; in the 'half leather' style, besides having a leather-bound spine, leather covers the corners of the book. Full leather binding is precisely what the term implies, the book being completely enclosed in leather. In the case of the quarter, half or full leather, the ridges seen on the spine of the book are called 'raised bands'. These are in fact the actual cords with which the book has been sewn. That cord is laced into the boards and it holds the boards and the

*Making a slip-case*

*Left: passing a slip-case cover through the whole-surface glueing machine*

book together. There are twenty-five or thirty operations involved in binding a book of this quality requiring a high degree of skill and patience from the craftsman.

Any craftsman finds satisfaction in the preservation of examples of his work, and in this respect the fine bookbinder is more fortunate than many. 'There are some of our bindings in the homes of members of the Royal Family', says Ken Smith. Presentation volumes have been bound and presented to the Queen, to Prince Philip (a specially bound copy of his book *Competition Carriage Driving*), and to Prince Charles and the Queen Mother (a production relating to Clarence House).

His work is nothing if not varied. So far, the largest book Smith Settle have bound is a monograph on the endangered rhinoceros, measuring 26½ inches by 19½, priced at the best part of £1,700 for the deluxe version (with which the purchaser receives an original painting). The smallest is a beautifully made hand-sewn book about two inches square on the subject of bookbinding, selling for about £30. Its author is the designer bookbinder Angela James.

The books in which Ken Smith personally takes greatest pride are *Four Poems* by Rupert Brook, quarter-bound in vellum during his days with Scolar Press and printed on hand-made paper, a book of

William Morris's verse with facsimile binding, a presentation bound copy of the manuscript of Milton's *Paradise Lost* for the University of Cambridge and *The Mirror and the Eye* from *The Rubaiyat of Omar Khayyám* in full leather, with leather inlays, illustrated by Richard Kennedy.

He is keen to acknowledge his indebtness to the Scolar Press, who, he says, gave him the opportunity to develop the skills on which Smith Settle has been built and to enlarge his knowledge of bibliography. Smith Settle itself, he is quick to acknowledge, owes as much to his partner and former colleague at Scolar Press, Brian Settle, as it does to him.

Would he encourage others to enter the industry in which he has found such success and satisfaction? 'I never do anything else,' he says, 'Undoubtedly, today, there's a shortage of traditional skills. The printing industry is moving very rapidly in terms of technological developments and standardisation and traditional companies such as ours tend not to attract so many would-be entrants. While there is no danger of traditional skills being lost altogether, there has been a contraction over the years in the size of binderies and fewer people are learning to practice traditional hand methods. We at Smith Settle, perhaps to a degree unique in Yorkshire, have established ourselves as traditional binders, whilst other people have tended to go in for more and more technology and rapid expansion.'

It is difficult to imagine a time when printing will have been completely superseded. It appears to be a craft rooted in history, witness Smith Settle's involvement in the binding of *The County Edition* of the *Domesday Facsimile*. The Yorkshire edition, complete with a set of folio maps, which costs about £260, has virtually sold out. 'That's the most popular of all, which is understandable', says Ken Smith.

There speaks a Yorkshireman. Even so, besides a marginal interest in publishing books with a Yorkshire flavour under their own imprint, this company of dedicated craftsmen is gaining a reputation throughout the world.

# Strong ale in Yorkshire

## Peculier brewing at Masham

*Oh Yorkshire, Yorkshire, thy ale is so strong*
*That it will kill us all if we stay long.*
*So they agreed a journey for to make*
*Into the South some respite to take.*

George Meriton, 1684

Mention Old Peculier, and any Yorkshireman who's heard of beer will say, 'Oh yes, Theakston!' But not many of them could tell you how this name for a famous beer arose. They will, however, all agree that if Theakston traditional ales are 'peculier' they are so in the true, original sense of being special.

The word 'peculier', whether you spell it with an E or an A, has changed its meaning somewhat since it was introduced, probably by the Normans. Its original meaning, and one of the primary definitions still given to the word in the Oxford Dictionary is 'exclusive'. But how did the word first become associated with Masham in Wensleydale? The beer has been brewed there since 1827 by the Theakston family, who probably first arrived in the Dales as Viking raiders in the tenth century.

A century or so later, Roger de Mowbray, Lord of the Manor hereabouts, took a body of Dalesmen to the crusades. He was captured by Saladin, the great Moslem leader, and did not get home until the Knights Templar ransomed him seven years later. As an act of gratitude to God, Roger de Mowbray gave the rich living of Masham and district to the Archbishop of York. And because the wild land between Masham and York was notorious for cut-throats, he set up a special (or 'peculier') court in Masham to deal with trouble-makers and administer the law generally. Hence the word, peculier, was oft used in the area and seemed appropriate for one of Theakston's most popular ales.

Theakston is one of the most indigenous of Dales concerns. Its story began when Robert Theakston, a farmer's son, and his friend John Wood took over the lease of a Masham pub and brewhouse, the

*Theakston's Brewery has a rural air which enables it to blend unobtrusively into the Wensleydale village of Masham*

*Bygone days at Masham*

*Manhandling hop sacks which contain one of the principal ingredients of beer*

Black Bull. Robert married John's sister, Eleanor, and after John died in 1832, Robert and Eleanor ran the business together. Customers must have multiplied, because in the early 1870s. The Black Bull brewhouse could no longer deal with the demand; so a new one was built which is still in use, along with the open slate fermenting vessels. Indeed, little seems to have changed in this brewery since it was opened, except that instead of an open fire, steam coils now supply heat.

As the years passed, each generation of the family added to the tradition. It was the grandsons of the founder, Robert and Edwin Theakston, who decided to make the brewery a limited company in 1905. The first World War called Robert from Masham and brewing for a while, but after his return in 1919, he and his brother Edwin took over the competing Lightfoot's brewery, famous not only for its nine pubs but for its cricket team! The two companies were hardly strangers, for Robert's mother – going back two generations to the time of the founder – had been born Mary Lightfoot.

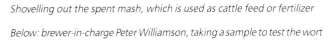

Edwin retired in the 1930s, but the brewbooks he used in the 1890s are still preserved. They prove how little the basic brews have changed over the years. Today, T & R Theakston Ltd is run as an independent company within the Scottish and Newcastle Group. Theakston is not only a highly successful and old-established company but a popular place for Dales tourists with a splendidly appointed, oak-furnished visitor centre, where award-winning videos are shown telling the Theakston story. Even more fascinating to most visitors is a 'live' exhibit they may watch through a window as the coopers demonstrate their skill of producing the traditional oak casks still in use at Masham. And it's not suprising that many visitors to Theakston's find barrels and the process of making them almost as interesting as their contents!

But before beer can be barrelled, it must of course be brewed. I talked about this to Peter Williamson, brewer in charge. Asked to describe a typical day in his life, he declared himself a jack of all trades (certainly of all the brewing trade), able to turn his hand to any part of the complex process which results in the pint at your elbow. In emergencies he might find himself 'mashing' in the early hours of the morning or staying late in the evening to 'collect' the brew, that is, to bring it to the correct gravity, which must be declared in the Excise Book.

Peter finds wry humour in the fact that he started in the industry, in Scotland, on December 31st, Hogmanay! He began as a laboratory assistant, weighing full and empty casks, and soon progressed to research chemist, spending five years as 'a backroom boffin' before moving into production departments. His experience has qualified him perfectly to answer questions from people who talk glibly about 'chemical beer'. Beer, of course, has always been 'chemical' in the sense that most things, you and me included, are chemical, being composed of chemical substances; but thanks to modern science, the hundreds of components, some at minute levels, that make up beer can be identified, measured and to some extent in modern brewing, controlled, to preserve the desired qualities of flavour and aroma. At Masham it is the individual skills of the brewing team which preserve the quality.

When all is said and done, Peter is pleased that Theakston's brew is ranked, by enthusiasts, high in the traditional, 'real ale' category. 'We welcome the interest of CAMRA (campaign for real ale) and any other lovers of ale', he said.

As brewer in charge, Peter has the responsibility of maintaining output and quality and of ensuring the safety of the workforce. Scotsman though he is, he refuses to involve himself in disputes about the respective virtues of Scottish and English beer, insisting that 'brewing is brewing' (and therefore, presumably, beer is beer). But what qualities, I persisted, make great beer, like Old Peculier? Good brewing, said Peter, is simply a matter of exercising unstinted care in the treatment of the best raw materials – the finest quality ingredients: malt, hops, sugar and yeast. If any trade secrets lie hidden in Edwin Theakston's brewbooks, they will remain secrets as far as Peter's concerned. Certainly he was giving nothing away when he said, 'We pride ourselves on quality'.

Brewing begins with the crushing of malt through a malt mill, and elevating it into a hopper (known as the 'grist case') over the mash tun, a circular vessel with a false bottom of slotted plates. Here the malt and hot liquor [water] are mixed into a 'mash' which is allowed to stand for about an hour and a half, during which the starch in the malt changes into sugar. Then the malt extract [the 'wort'] is run off from the bottom of the mash tun to the 'copper' while hot liquor, sprayed over the top of the grains in the mash tun, carries the wort through the copper. There the whole brew is boiled for 1¾ hrs while concentrated sugars and the best English hops are added.

When the boiling is completed the brew is cast into the 'hop back', which filters the spent hops from the brew. From the hop back the wort is pumped up into a cooler, where it stands for a short time before being run through a wort paraflow [cooling system] to bring down the temperature to 62°F. After cooling, the brew is collected in the fermenting vessel and the yeast is added.

This is when, in layman's terms, the mash, mixture, brew, starts to become what we know as beer. Due to the action of the yeast feeding on the sugars, alcohol and carbon dioxide are produced and the yeast cells multiply to form a white frothy

*Waiting to take away the spent mash by lorry as it emerges from the chute*

head. After about three days, when this has reached its peak, the excess yeast is skimmed off, all except for a thin crust which is allowed to remain as a shield against airborne moulds and bacteria. For a further few days the fermentation is left and cooled to 55°F. The beer is racked off into wooden casks direct from the fermenting vessel.

Clive Hollis, head cooper, is properly proud of his craft. It calls not only for skill but for strength and proficiency in the handling of a multitude of tools, many of them virtually antiques, such as heading knives, bow saws, augers and adzes. These have served generations of coopers whose initials on them bear witness to their craftsmanship.

In the present technological age a barrel may appear a simple object. But Theakston, proud of their coopering tradition, point out that 'barrels' are mentioned in the Bible. Indeed, vessels of a clearly similar type were made in Egypt as early as 2690 BC. For thousands of years, in fact, mankind relied on barrels for the storage or transportation of goods. Barrels were strong, they were secure, and, being round, could be rolled instead of lifted, no matter how big they were.

Though coopers at one time made buckets, washing bowls, churns for butter and tubs for cheese, it was the spread of brewing, after the arrival

*Filling a wooden barrel*

*Head cooper Clive Hollis assembles a barrel end, a task which requires great accuracy of hand and eye*

of beer from the Low Countries in about 1490, that offered the biggest market for the cooper's skill.

Today there are probably fewer than a dozen coopers left in this country, Mr Hollis is one of a vanishing band. He started work as an apprentice straight from school at Burton-on-Trent, he signed his indentures on his sixteenth birthday and completed his apprenticeship the day he was twenty-one, undergoing the same initiation as former Theakston apprentice Alastair Simms. Clive believes Theakston has the last apprentice in the brewing industry. And a sad fact that seems when you reflect on the incredible skill, learned by sheer practice and thus experience, that goes into making a cask.

First the timber has to be cut to the required length and thickness, then the stave has to be 'listed', that is, roughly shaped, the longer staves on an instrument called a block, the shorter ones on a device known as a 'donkey'. The actual shaping is done with an axe. Next the staves are jointed by means of a very long upturned plane [the 'jointer']. The jointing, which holds the staves together in the cask, has to be perfect so that no liquid leaks out under pressure.

The cooper then looks carefully down each jointed stave to judge the degree of 'belly' he is putting in the cask, using judgement based on years of experience. When enough staves have been dressed they are joined with hoops to form a cask and immersed in a steam bath to soften the timber and make it more pliable. Smaller hoops are then affixed to pinch the cask in at the ends, and it is next placed over a fire in a cresset [metal basket] to 'set' the staves. The cask is then 'chimbed', in other words, a bevel or slope is cut on the ends of the staves to form the rim.

Every one of these processes has to be water-tight in the most literal sense and after each operation the cask under construction is rigorously tested. To ensure that the chimbs [ends] are square, a topping plane is used; while to make certain that the cask is perfectly carved, so that a groove may be cut in it to take the head, the cooper uses a tool called a 'chiv', resting the developing cask between his knees and the block. Other ancient tools are also employed, including a 'croze', which actually cuts the groove at each end of the barrel. To make sure that there are no crevices where bacteria might lurk, the inside of the cask is shaved smooth so it can be effectively sterilised.

Next, by using compasses around the groove, the cooper ascertains the size of the head required. The pieces that make up the head are joined together with wooden dowels inserted in holes cut with a brace held against the cooper's chest. Before he uses his hammer to tap home the connecting pieces of the head, he inserts a piece of rush or flag into the joints. On contact with liquid, this will swell and ensure that the cask is perfectly sealed.

Both sides of both heads are shaved with a 'swift' before the hoops around the cask are slackened to permit the heads to be affixed from inside and located in the grooves. A tool called a downright and another called a buzz are used to smooth the outside of the cask. When the hoops have been driven back into place, the cask is complete.

Cask making has a small language all of its own, though some of its terms have passed into common usage. So while the names of tools used by coopers may sound mysterious, the names of the casks themselves are more familiar. They range from the largest, the butt, 108 gallons, via the hogshead, 54 gallons, barrel, 36 gallons, kilderkin, 18 gallons, the firkin, 9 gallons, to the pin, 4.5 gallons.

It is the hogshead which plays a part in the cheerful if somewhat messy ceremony which marks the emergence of the fully trained cooper. Having

*The cooper's shop where craftsmen practise one of the most ancient of skills, barrel and cask making, is an unfailing source of interest to visitors*

made his hogshead, minus the 'heads', the apprentice 'just out of his time', is placed inside it and the staves which form the walls of the barrel are bent around him. Then, Clive Hollis explained, 'You pour over him whatever you like – beer, yeast, shavings, anything at all. You hand him his indentures and then all have a drink together.'

Theakston are proud of their share in maintaining the wonderful old craft of coopering. This is probably the last brewery in the United Kingdom to have an apprentice cooper, though they are still to be found in the whisky distilleries of Scotland. There is no doubting that Clive Hollis has enjoyed the job he has worked at all his life, though as the exponent of a vanishing craft, he has, he says, 'had to follow the work' and settled in Masham, where the scenery reminds him so much of his native Derbyshire.

Altogether, there is much to delight visitors to Theakston, not least, if they're lucky, a glimpse of the restored dray, built at the turn of the century, with its cargo of Masham-made casks. The dray is drawn by two magnificent grey shires, Dane and General, driven by Julie Mills, who has been showing horses for ten years. Incidentally, both these giants have acquired a keen taste for Theakston's beer. Need you ask which kind? The strongest of course – Old Peculier!

*Peculier sign outside the Bruce Arms, Tanfield, Wensleydale*

EST. 1827

SEAL OF THE OFFICIAL OF THE PECULIER OF MASHAM 1741

**THEAKSTON**
TRADITIONAL ALES

Bruce Arms

# Black beauty

Whitby jet

At one time it was probably easier to get a Whitby smuggler to give you a timetable of his dealings in contraband than to get a jet carver to tell you how he worked the lustrous black stuff into shapes beloved of Queen Victoria and her subjects with special tools, most of which were made by hand. As for taking pictures of these sacrosanct processes by which he produced the glittering, many-faceted objects so admired by his customers, you might as well ask permission to photograph the afore-mentioned Queen Victoria in her bath. It was a secretive business, jet. You'd hear stories of jet carvers studying the latest contents of each other's shop windows at dead of night, with the aid of torches.

Surprisingly few of the present-day practitioners are Whitby-born and bred. One who is, Roy Jay, has been a jet carver for over thirty years and believes himself to have been the last of his dusty trade to have served a full apprenticeship in the time-honoured tradition. Fortunately, Roy is less cagey than some of his predecessors or this chapter might never have been written.

One of a family already dealing in gifts, books and jewellery, Roy, as a lad, became acquainted with 'an old guy, a hermit' living at nearby Ruswarp, called Jack Harrison, who used to bring his jet carvings to the family shop and offer them for sale. Young Roy found himself strangely attracted by old Jack's intricately carved cuff links, necklaces, bracelets and brooches: 'I was fascinated by how he made his facets and cuts and one night, when he visited the house, I asked him how he did it.'

Listening to the conversation, Roy's father could sense that his son's questions were prompted by more than mere curiosity. 'You seemed interested in what old Jack had to say, son,' he remarked, when Jack was on his way home to Ruswarp. 'Do you fancy doing something like that for a living?' And Roy, whose pet subject at school had always been art, was nothing loth.

There were three qualified jet carvers alive in Whitby at that time and only two of those were practising their craft. One of these was Joe Lyth and the other Wilf Braithwaite, both known for years by visitors to Whitby's quaintly named Khyber Pass, where both had their workshops. Joe Lythe, when approached by Roy's father, agreed to take the lad on as an apprentice, but before Roy left school old Joe died. So it was the other craftsman, Wilf Braithwaite, a specialist in pearl inlay, who taught the fourteen year old all he knew during the evenings and at weekends, whenever Wilf could spare the time from his post as one of the living relics of old Whitby.

In the 1960s, after five years of learning everything old Wilf could teach him, Roy set up business on his own account as a jet carver. At that time, in Roy's words, the trade in jet, which had never recovered the popularity it had enjoyed in Victorian times, was 'just ticking over'. Then in the mid-sixties, Roy ventured into more modernistic designs and this produced a flurry of interest which to some extent has been maintained. But nowadays, says Roy, because too many customers 'expect the results of two days work for five or six quid'. Some jet workers tend to lean away from the richly carved and faceted work to what he calls 'basic stuff', for example what is apparently known in lapidary circles as the 'Caversham' [cabochon] a polished, domed stone which might be used in a ring or a pendant.

Because he is a craftsman who knows there will always be a market for fine, painstaking work, Roy still works on carved and faceted original pieces. As well as making copies of Victorian jewellery. His raw material is found locally, picked up on the beach by 'jetties', who may have taken a day off from fishing in the hope of finding a rich seam of jet in the cliffs to sell to Whitby's carvers at anything from £8 - £15 per pound. Time was when men could work full time and make a decent living from jet gathering, but most work part-time today.

*Church Street, in one of the older parts of Whitby, where jet working was once a staple trade*

Holiday-makers, too, often find jet – or think they do, but a good deal of what is optimistically offered for the carvers' inspection turns out to be glass, coal, vulcanite or even plastic – anything, in fact, but jet. What is known as 'washed jet' can be carried ashore by the sea anywhere between Bridlington and Saltburn during rough weather, when pieces are broken away from seams in the bituminous shales extending beneath the sea between Robin Hood's Bay and Boulby. For millennia, jet deposits lay hidden beneath the earth miles inland until the glacier which scored out the Esk Valley carried a three-mile portion of the shales seaward.

*Above: a nineteenth century jet workshop in Haggergate, Whitby, photographed by Frank Meadow Sutcliffe. This was the only jet workshop equipped with gas-engine powered lathes*

*Left: 'That looks interesting' . . . Jack Crock, a present-day 'jetty', beachcombing at Whitby*

When Roy started in business the top price would be about 2 shillings per pound. But there's an awful lot of waste, he says, in raw jet, and the usable material is dramatically reduced in quantity by the time it has been cleansed of the adhering shale. But what, precisely, is jet? Geologists have declared it to be a form of carbon or coal. However, craftsmen who have worked with both jet and amber have expressed the belief that the two substances were similarly formed millions of years ago when sap flowed down the trunks of giant trees to solidify and await discovery by man, who named the black or golden stuff jet or amber. The existence of stones completely surrounded by jet, as well as fossil impressions on the surface of the seams, would appear to support this theory.

There is 'hard' jet and 'soft' jet, Roy explains: 'When the demand for the jet articles was at its

greatest, a lot of soft jet was used, and this, unlike the hard jet, was prone to dry out and crack. In days before the Trades Description Act, carvers might use varieties of coal or even bog-wood; the important thing was that it should be black.'

Jet is found in many parts of the world, but in Yorkshire at least it is believed that the best hard jet is found within the Broad Acres. One thing seems certain: it took the Yorkshiremen of Whitby to fully exploit the commercial and artistic possibilities of the 'black stuff' found on their coast and (with the help of Queen Victoria) make it the basis of a thriving industry.

But they did not discover jet, for the working of it dates back to Roman times, and long before. In the 10,000-year-old burial barrows of Bronze-Age folk, roughly cut beads, placed there to ward off evil spirits, reveal that long before Victoria reigned, jet was associated with funeral rites. The Romans wore jet bracelets, rings and medallions, as evidenced by discoveries at Yorkshire sites like Huntcliff and Normanby. And Chaucer mentions the bright black Yorkshire stone prized in his day by fourteenth-century followers of fashion.

Today the demand is still for rings, pendants, earrings. In the days when living was cheaper, before the advent of VAT and endlessly soaring rates, a carver could afford to work at his craft from perhaps six in the morning to five at night for a guinea a week. From the standpoint of craftsmanship, those were the great days. The workers would never be rich, but at least they made a living and could dream of one day producing a masterpiece, like a piece much admired by Roy in Whitby Museum – a head of Christ crowned with thorns.

Most jet workers make their own equipment – and can be remarkably secretive about it. Roy admits you, without hesitation, to his workshop in the upper reaches of a two hundred-year-old building in Whitby's Church Street; to reach it you have to climb winding staircases in the dark, and heed Roy's warnings to mind your head. More than one TV camera crew, he says, have found themselves in difficulties negotiating obstacles separating them from the dusty haven where powdered jet floats like smoke in the sunlight. Here Roy's lathes and 'mills' are offered for your inspection while he tells you the difference between 'turning' and

faceting and recalls the bygone 'good lads' who could get as many as 'sixty-four canters [facets] on a bead. Imagine having fifty beads on a necklace, with sixty-four facets on each bead. It would sparkle beautifully!'

Methods very from carver to carver, but generally speaking, the first task is to 'chop out' the material into sizes suitable for working, using a tungsten steel chisel with a weighted handle. Next the pieces are ground more closely to the required shape on a grindstone. Various processes follow, including the use of a wheel made in a frying pan with melted lead, tin and antimony!

The medieval alchemists could hardly have had a more remarkable range of equipment. There are brushes and wheels ranging from six inches to a foot in diameter. There is a pig's bristle brush fed with 'rotten stone' [a fine abrasive river mud from Derbyshire] and water. There is the 'listing board', usually made from woollen rags wound round a wooden core, yet another wheel made of pure wool strips, a rouge wheel and rouge board. During each process, each piece of jet is handled perhaps a dozen times. And in addition to all this there are three

processes, each of which at one time would have been the specialised task of one man – carving, beadmaking and inlaying. Even now I have given no more than the briefest outline of a craft but even a slight acquaintance with it should help to explain its fascination for its practitioners.

When Roy, by rubbing a piece of jet in his workshop, created a thin, smoke like effect, I found it easy to understand why jet was at one time believed to have magical properties which could be used to lift spells, remove the effects of the evil eye or repel old Nick himself – who was presumably nonplussed to be confronted by something even blacker than himself! When a woman accused of witchcraft had been cast out of her home in Egton, not far from Whitby, in about 1807, a cross made of jet was placed across her door to prevent her returning.

The first Whitby jet workers were probably a painter and an inn-keeper who, in about 1800, turned out rough beads and crosses with the aid of knives and files. The idea of turning jet on a lathe never occurred to them until an old sailor who had seen amber similarly treated introduced it to them.

*The grinding of jet produces a very fine dust which endangers the lungs, hence the mask worn here by Roy*

Queen Victoria's share in promoting the wearing of jet would be hard to exaggerate. After the death of her consort Prince Albert, she wore great quantities of jet jewellery, with amazing effects on the jet trade. If they had planned it, the jet workers could hardly have found a greater boost for their sales. Albert died in 1861 and ten years later the Whitby jet industry was employing 1,500 men, women and children whose products found ready customers at home and throughout the world.

The Victorians, it is often said, were in love with death. Later generations had different predilections. Indeed it was the very association with mourning which had given jet its boom period, that reduced it to its present proportions. Even before the unprecedented carnage of the first World War, the public seem to have fallen out with the sombre or sentimental celebration of mortality. Black was no longer the 'in' colour, and so the trade in jet declined.

Somewhere in the Pontiff's personal quarters in the Vatican there is probably a cross of carved Whitby jet by Roy Jay. It was handed to Pope John Paul by a Whitby boy, one of a group making a visit to the Vatican. Roy's work has been presented also to Prince Charles (a solid silver paper knife with a jet handle in the shape of a fisherman's head), to Princess Diana (a bracelet), Princess Margaret (jet-mounted silver coffee and tea spoons), The Duke of Gloucester (cuff links) and the Duchess (a model in jet of Whitby Abbey), while the Duchess of Kent received a pendant.

The biggest single article Roy has carved is probably a model of Fylingdales Early Warning Station presented to Colonel Hunt, then Commanding Officer, on his return to the USA. The smallest and certainly one of the most intricate pieces was Lord Londonderry's seal in a silver finger ring.

Jet certainly has a past, but what of it's future? As long as Whitby attracts visitors, some of them will consider it almost obligatory to take home a piece of Whitby jet, just as visitors to Derbyshire will take home a piece of the indigenous blue-john stone. The possibilities of extending the market by commercialising jet production leave Roy

*A miniature table and chair set, with decanters, chessboard and an engraving of Whitby Abbey on the table.*

unenthusiastic. He has no wish, he says, to 'cheapen' his craft. 'If you're turning out quantity, then your quality goes. I wasn't taught that way. I was taught to do a job and the job takes time. No matter what I do I can't quicken it up.' Neither does the prospect of employing others to do the work appeal to him.

Would he, in due time, feel like handing on his knowledge to others, such as his two sons? He is quite philosophical about the fact that neither of them, not even 'the arty one', has the slightest intention of following in his steps. 'They don't want to be in business at all and they don't want to work as I've had to work, seven days a week.' That does not surprise him. 'You're locked in a little room. It's a filthy job with a lot of dust. You have to wear a surgical mask, as I have since 1967, when I got a blocked lung through my work.' He has had no lung trouble since then, because, despite the fineness of the dust, it cannot penetrate his double pad surgical mask.

One of Roy's few regrets is that he was not born fifty or so years earlier in the great days of jet carving, before it became prohibitive for a jet carver to lavish many hours on an inlaid cameo head on a ring; when there were many men like Roy's mentor, Wilf Braithwaite, turning out superbly faceted masterpieces. Who knows? Perhaps some day another lad in love with jet's black beauty will ask to learn Roy's secrets. I hope so, because skill like his deserves to be cherished.

# Little Mesters

## Skill with steel in Sheffield

Kelham Island may seem an unlikely name to find in the heart of Sheffield. Hardly surprising, then, that in as productive a place as Sheffield, the 'island' is man-made, a remnant of the city's industrial past and, as a leaflet tells you, is the site of a magnificent monument to Sheffield's history: 'It is a museum where the past meets the present and history is alive'.

Indeed, some of the actual exhibits are very much alive – and working. These are the 'Little Mesters', four craftsmen in the cutlery industry who practise their traditional skills as self-employed businessmen in workshops recreated within the museum's walls. The term 'little mester' (little master) was coined to distinguish the one- or two-man businesses from the big Sheffield factories employing hundreds.

As Rowland Swinden, a grinder, explained, 'Before the museum opened, we all had our individual workshops in Sheffield. It was decided that the museum authorities would like three little mesters to work in the museum.' As things turned out, the three finally became four and the basis of their agreement was that the museum would provide workshops at a low rent in return for the craftsmen putting themselves on public display. That seemed 'a fair exchange' to Rowland and his fellows, and after ten years as exhibits they seem to have no regrets.

Originally the Little Mesters each followed a very specific trade. Grinders, such as Rowland, specialised in his early days in the trade in performing a distinct role in the production of a particular article. 'You were a grinder of pocket-knives, or penknives, or Bowie knives' (murderous-looking implements beloved of collectors and named after Colonel Jim Bowie, a legendary hero of the old West), or table knives, chisels, scrapers or pallets (flat blades used by potters). However, as machine-grinding became more and more the accepted method, hand-grinders

*Rowland Swinden (left) and Graham Clayton at the doors of their Kelham Island workshops*

*Inset: entrance to Kelham Island Industrial Museum, Sheffield*

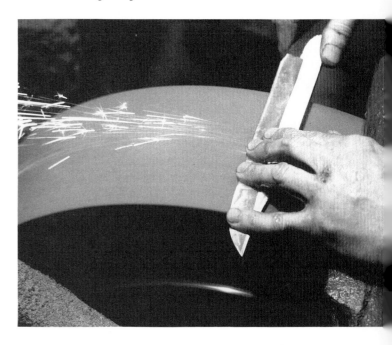

were no longer trained in the craft. 'All the older ones died off', said Rowland, 'or lost their jobs for one reason or another. This meant that the few of us who were left started doing anything that came into the workshop instead of one specific job. That's how it is today.'

*Rowland Swinden grinding*

Little Mesters still in business, says Rowland, including cutlers and forgers, total a dozen at the outside. But the term lives on due to its application to a variety of trades, including self-employed engineers. The original Little Mesters were skilled men, who, having been employed by the big steel masters, realised that they would make more money by selling their products, rather than their labour, and broke away from the big companies to set up their own businesses, eventually becoming small employers themselves. With the inevitable advance of mechanisation, the big 'mesters' told their lesser brothers, 'Thanks, lads, but we've got a machine that can do your job'. But still the little men survived,

because there were always smaller orders coming into the big shops, which could be done more cheaply by hand.

There are still jobs which cannot adequately be done by machinery. As examples, Rowland showed me the blades of swords and Bowie knives lying on a bench awaiting his attention. As long as work of this quality has to be done, he believes, the Little Mesters will have a place.

Rowland's workshop has only existed in its present form for ten years, but it looks much older. 'We keep it a bit scruffy', he confided, 'because we were asked to make it look like an original little mesters' grinding shop!'

Visitors to Kelham Island total about 50,000 a year and inevitably they are fascinated by this little colony of craftsmen. Through the windows of the specially created workshop they can watch the Little Mesters at work, and during moments when they are engaged on tasks which don't require unbroken concentration, the craftsmen perform a feat far beyond the reach of most museum exhibits by answering questions about themselves and their work.

Rowland has in his time trained an apprentice who now also works as a Little Mester, but he sees no prospect of anyone following in his footsteps at the museum. 'A one-man business nowadays, can't afford to train apprentices', he explains. Only if the council were able to compensate the craftsman for what he lost by training a successor would it be possible to ensure that this remarkable example of truly living history could continue.

Practices vary in the different trades, but a day in the life of this particular Little Mester would go along these lines. Newly forged, hardened and tempered blades are first of all delivered to Rowland from the forge. Usually his morning task is to grind the blades – possibly half-a-dozen Bowie knives, together with some pocket-knife or penknife blades

– to the sharpness required, but lacking the mirror gloss that is expected by the customer.

In the afternoon he finishes the blades by means of a glazing wheel which eliminates the marks left by the grinding process. After using a second glazing wheel which heightens the finish, a 'felt mop' and then a 'calico mop' are put to work. These glazing wheels are virtually museum pieces in themselves, having been handed down in Rowland's family from generation to generation. They are made of wood rimmed by leather. The leather is dressed with a mixture of glue and emery. In all there are five operations performed on blades received from the forge – first grinding, which Rowland compares to the application of a very rough sandpaper to wood, then rough glazing, involving a slightly finer abrasive. The process advances by the use of increasingly finer abrasives until the polishing stage is reached.

Undoubtedly the most impressive of Rowland's gleaming products are the swords and Bowie knives produced mostly for collectors. 'This is a replica of a First World War smachete', he said, handing me a vicious-looking implement resembling an outsize spear-head with handle attached, which was apparently used in hand-to-hand trench warfare. An all-purpose tool if ever I saw one, it could be used for digging, chopping and, of course, for its primary purpose – killing. It was destined for an American customer who sent a drawing of the required article, which was then faithfully followed. So besides working for the big cutlery companies in their home city of Sheffield, these Little Mesters are constantly demonstrating the ancient skills of the one-time cutlery capital to the world.

In another corner of the workshop there was an English broadsword replica, possibly destined for a museum. 'Last week I made half-a-dozen sword-dancers' swords for a museum up in the North-East', said Rowland. Like so many other craftsmen, he finds that some of his most difficult tasks are what the layman might consider the easiest – repairs: 'They'll ask me to remove a chip from a blade, while making sure the finished article looks as if it has remained untouched during its century or whatever of existence. Apart from the actual difficulty and time-consuming nature of such jobs there is always the possible incredulity of the customer when the bill

*Peter Goss hand-forging surgical instruments*

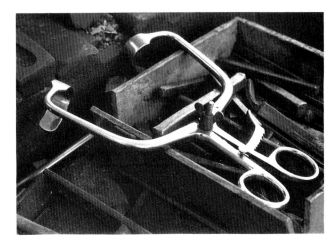
*Retractors, used in surgery to hold back flesh*

has to be paid. They could very often buy a new knife for what it costs to repair the old one.'

Rowland, who left school at fourteen in 1946, was apprenticed to his uncle until he was twenty-one. After National Service he stayed with his uncle for a further couple of years before joining Joseph Rodgers, then the biggest cutlery firm in the world.

It was the custom at the time for such large concerns to invite competent practitioners to 'rent a trow' from them, which consisted in Rowland's case of a grindstone and a glazing wheel. The manufacturers would then provide the grinder with work and employ him on a piecework basis. Rowland stayed with Rodgers for about seventeen years, after which he rented a workshop and became, in the fullest sense, a Little Mester.

Peter Goss, one of Rowland's colleagues in this little enclave of Sheffield's industrial past, is a surgical instrument forger. His raw material was straight bars of steel which, in finished form, was destined to enter many hundreds of human mouths as a dental spatula. This, a fairly simple example of his craft, according to Peter, was the sort of job that might be entrusted to 'a lad' to make. Asked to produce something from the opposite extreme, he showed me a tonsillectomy instrument which it might be advisable to examine after, rather than before you undergo the operation in which it is employed. Operated in a scissor-like action, its cylindrical blade deftly slices off the unwanted organ.

Peter Goss has followed his calling for thirty-six years and is now the only man working at his craft by hand. Despite their delicacy, he estimates that perhaps 99.5 per cent of surgical instruments are

stamped out of the steel. Did he feel that his instruments were produced to a higher standard than those made by modern, high-speed methods. His answer was an unequivocal, if surprising 'No. The only advantage hand-forging would have is in the case of a knife blade or other instrument with a cutting edge, where the constant striking of the metal closes the molecules together, to produce a harder and better edge. In the case of just an ordinary surgical instrument there is no advantage whatsoever.'

One reason Peter is unlikely ever to be out of work is that it is uneconomical to stamp small quantities of any item, so as he is the only one of his kind he gets a steady stream of small orders.

Will he be the last of his breed? That depends on whether, to use his words, he can 'find a lad that will take to it.' In a few years he hopes to pass on his craft, but so far he has nobody particular in mind. Such a lad would have to be cast in the same mould as

Peter himself, who readily took to his craft because he 'enjoyed making things'.

No less taciturn than the average Sheffield craftsman, Peter allows some enjoyment in his work to shine through as he says, 'I like to see the end product when it's all working and shining'. I hope he's successful in finding the lad who will be fortunate enough to share that enthusiasm.

Graham Clayton was apprenticed as a spring-knife cutler for six years during which he mostly learned the art and science of making pocket knives, but after a couple of years with two other firms he set up on his own account in 1974 because he wanted to work mostly 'in the collectors' market' and 'rather than make, say, a couple of gross of three-bladed pocket knives a week I would make two or three special items'.

The home of the knife collector is primarily in the USA, though interest is growing rapidly in Britain. The most collected item is the Bowie knife, along

*Left: Peter Goss using a 'nodding donkey' hammer*

*Above: Graham Clayton hammers away in similar style!*

with folding knives, in which the blade fits into the handle, jack-knife fashion. Some of these are beautifully ornamented with pearl-covered shafts, and can cost £110 and more. 'They're totally hand-made from start to finish', says Graham who starts his task with 'just a piece of steel and a piece of pearl – pearl is the expensive part', but no doubt customers feel its scintillating effect fully justifies the expense.

The most expensive collectors' item Graham has so far made was a three-bladed knife about nine inches long with gold ends instead of the usual nickel. 'It worked out at about £830 to the customer but there was £450 of gold in it. The large piece of pearl was expensive and there was about £100 worth of engraving on it, so by the time it was finished I'd made no more than I would on a normal one, but it was nice to have made it.'

He has made even larger three-bladers which, when closed, measured perhaps twenty-four inches long, and when open, about forty inches. The dimensions prompt the question whether such large implements are truly usable, but as Graham explains, 'These are just display pieces.' A particularly large and impressive Bowie knife that would surely have made Colonel Bowie himself blink was destined, said Graham, for a collector who was a lumberjack in British Columbia and described himself as 'a mountain man'. The splendid hilt of this knife is made from the 'crown' of an Indian samba deer's antlers. This is the part situated in the skull and from which the antlers grow and from which they drop when shed; it is also the most expensive part of the antlers.

Graham not only delights in making such exotic cutlery, he has also studied its history. 'In the 1870s', he says, 'the days of the old Wild West, these were fighting knives, wielded even by the West's wild

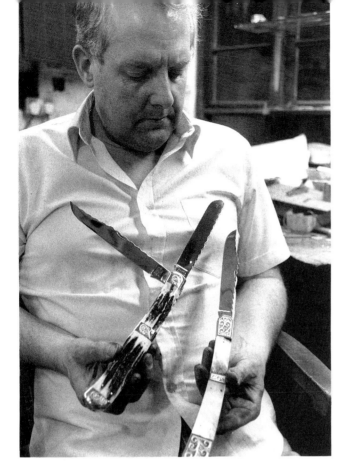

*Above: Graham Clayton with two of his folding knives made for collectors at home and abroad. The two-bladed knife has a stag's horn handle, the single-bladed one a pearl handle*

*Left: not just a 'hammer-man' – it is the wide range of skills needed that adds to Graham's job satisfaction and makes him a true craftsman*

women, such as Calamity Jane, who are shown in old photographs wearing them in their belts, just like the men. They were all-purpose items, used not only for fighting but for skinning, and for chopping wood for the camp fire. In the really early days you were probably armed with a one-shot musket. If you fired at an attacking bear and failed to stop it, you'd no time to re-load, so all you had left to defend yourself with was your knife.'

The weapon I was admiring had a twelve-inch blade, but Graham, with his keen historical sense, is rather a purist in such matters, so prefers the ten-inch blade as being more in keeping with the realities of the violent past which gave rise to the Bowie knife.

Graham became established in this branch of his trade by visiting the USA, where knife shows are regularly held, and sometimes take over entire hotels. As a Sheffield man, indeed, he may not enjoy admitting 'there are more cutlery firms in America than here'. The knife shows apparently grew out of the gun shows which incidentally included knives, but which now, he says, have become 'knife shows

with the odd gun'. After giving three knife shows in the States in five years and receiving useful television publicity in Britain, he seems to have all the work he can handle, but says he would not refuse more.

Graham says he has no-one in mind as a possible successor, a situation he seems to share with most of his colleagues at Kelham Island's Little Mesters' colony. Sad as it seems, not only do the craftsmen seem to be heading towards retirement as the last of their lines, but their materials, too, are becoming scarcer.

'Stags' horn for knife handles is harder and harder to come by. Stainless steel and pearl are still OK – fortunately, the pearl cutter I use actually works in Sheffield.' One trade relies upon another, and so, if the engravers, the heat treatment specialists, the grinders, the forgers are decreasing in number, the other little mesters who rely upon them are also hindered. 'So if I brought a lad in here to follow after me, he'd be even worse off than I might finally be, some of the others are heading for retirement but I have another twenty years to go yet.'

Ken Ladley had manufactured surgical and dental instruments for fifty years when I met him and had been at Kelham Island for a little over three years. When he first started there after working virtually alone during most of his career, he found the presence of visitors rather disconcerting. Being the polite and pleasant character he is, he felt obliged, when interested visitors paused at his window, to stop work and chat. 'Eventually I realised this couldn't go on, because I was getting nothing done.' Now, if anybody taps on his window while he is working he will gladly stop and answer questions. Otherwise he gets on with the work in hand. Even two or three enquiries can take up a lot of time that is really needed for production, but Ken takes an all-round view of his situation and is generally very satisfied with his lot.

'They look after you at this place', he says. 'They're very good at getting repairs done to your machines. We work together – put it that way. After all, we are here because the visitors want to see how we work – the old fashioned way. I make dental extraction forceps by hand, five pairs a day. A large firm will probably mass produce a thousand a week. If you put the two together you might not notice any difference. But for me there's an individual feel to each instrument I make and I feel proud that I've made it.'

There speaks the true craftsman, a man with an unmistakable zest for a job that calls forth the special skills he has spent his life acquiring and in the exercise of which he excels. The thought of work on an assembly line, where little is called for beyond the ability to press a switch or pull a lever, fills him with horror and pity for those who have to endure it. 'My job has plenty of variety. I might be on t'bench doing a couple of hours fitting. When I get tired of that I'll do a bit of grinding, then I might do a bit of polishing. I arrange it so that I'm moving about all the time.'

Ken receives the newly forged instruments in their rough, black form from the hand-forger. 'I fit them up, grind them, machine them if necessary, then send them to be hardened and tempered by a firm which specialises in that, and when I get them back I polish them. So I do everything myself except the hardening and tempering.'

Would he follow the same calling if he were starting his life again? He thinks for a moment, then chuckles. 'Put it this way – I've never been bored with this job, but as for starting all over again . . . Up to twenty-five years ago there was bags of work for me to do, but during this last twenty years work has dropped off alarmingly, firms are closing all over the place and little people like us have to rely on other little people. I might have to refuse an order because although I could do my part, I couldn't find any-body to do the plating on carbon steel pliers that might be needed to finish the job. Nowadays it seems that everything we want has to come from Germany. It's really pathetic that a country like ours with our history in cutlery manufacture should have ended up like this.'

Ken has no apprentice to follow in his steps. He had one, but lost him to a big firm and now feels no inclination to repeat the experience. If, however, Sheffield City Council would pay an apprentice's wages, he would be fully prepared to do his best, during the last of his working years, to impart the skill and knowledge of a lifetime to some likely successor who, like him, valued the job satisfaction that his craft provides.

Training an apprentice from scratch cannot be easy. The most difficult thing to learn about Ken's work is, he says, 'bringing the component parts together, shaping it up and getting it ready for hardening. Everything has to be perfect or doctors and dentists won't accept them. And of course if they're not right it gives you a bad name anyway'.

The next step is grinding the implement to reduce the weight and make it easier to handle during the following stage, which is filing on the bench. And through all these processes care must be taken to ensure that what Ken calls 'a nice shape' is retained. 'This is the hardest thing', he insists. 'It takes longer to teach a chap that than anything else. At the same time, that's the most satisfying part of the work. When I was a young apprentice I used to find it really splendid that I could start a job one morning and pick it up at the end of the day and say. "I've made that." They don't get that satisfaction today – it's like a conveyor belt. A chap will do one job then pass it on to the next man. To me that's boring. So while a lot of the hard work has gone, so too has much of the interest.'

Ken feels he was fortunate to enter the trade while there were still many old men on the point of ending their careers who were willing to pass on to him, not only their enormous knowledge ('and by gum, they knew a lot', he says) but even some of their tools, tools which had probably been handed down to them and some of which he still uses today, though much of his specialised equipment he has made himself. And despite his regrets about some aspects of modern cutlery production, he readily admits that there have been many changes for the better since the days of 'grinders' asthma' when dust extraction plant was much less efficient and when factory inspectors were unknown. The work was much harder then, because everything was hand-forged, but hard times produce hard men, and women too, for those were the days of the 'buffer girls' with their prodigious energy and indomitable cheerfulness, whose task it was to polish the items to a mirror finish.

Ken takes satisfaction from the fact that during the twenty-five years he has been self-employed, his work has given him great enjoyment, which has continued, free from the stress and strain of running a business, by being based at Kelham Island.

*Ken Ladley shaping and fitting dental pliers*

# Broadside on

## Shipbuilders at Selby

When you have seen a ship launched at Selby, you don't forget it. In that ancient Abbey town there is no great expanse of water into which a newly built vessel can glide stern first. Instead, ships have to be launched 'broadside on' into the comparatively narrow River Ouse. And having slipped sideways into the water, the hull rolls ponderously over, almost as if about to capsize, before righting herself and sending a great wave towards the opposite bank.

Certainly the vagaries of the Ouse have to be considered by anyone presuming to build ships on her bank, notably her famously tight bends. Furthermore, she is tidal and runs at a fast current. But side-launching, though it has its problems, has even more advantages. With end-launching there is always a point at which part of the hull is on land and part in the water, causing stresses and possibly structural damage unless every factor has been meticulously calculated. This limits the amount of equipment which can be put on board before launching. With side-launching, however, stresses are evenly spread and so reduced that a vessel can virtually be fully assembled before she even touches the water.

Cochrane's are now one of the very few shipyards in Great Britain still launching by this method – a difficult one, the layman might think. To transfer thousands of tons of steel safely to the water from a flimsy-looking cradle seems difficult enough in any conditions, a task calling for judgement and a high degree of skill. But for anybody with a love of ships shipbuilding is a fascinating occupation. How could a naval architect like Eric Hammal, Design Manager and Naval Architect at Cochrane's, do his immensely detailed work to the life-and-death standards demanded if he were not stirred by the quiet passion shared by both the little boy sailing his craft on the park lake and the captain of an ocean liner?

*Preparing for a life at sea, a ship called Eliza is reflected in the smooth waters of the Yorkshire river*

During his twenty-eight years with Cochrane's the most significant developments Eric has seen have been the advent of computer-aided draughting and computerised technical calculation. But a more outward and visible sign of change at Selby is in the kind of ships built there. 'When I first came here, towards the end of the Cochrane family's era, we would never build longer than 200 feet. But as time goes on, you experiment and now we build up to 350 feet or 105–106 metres,' recalls Eric. And those spectacular sideways launches are in fact a blessing in disguise. For one thing, 'We don't have to worry about hitting the opposite bank as you would with end-launches across the river.'

Cochrane's shipyard was founded at Beverley in 1884 and moved to Selby in 1898. There were sufficient, indeed compelling reasons for the move. Only a couple of years earlier, almost £100,000 worth of profitable work had to be refused owing to lack of space at the Grovehill shipyard, Beverley, and they had a growing workforce of around 500 people. In 1899 the first launch at the new yard was recorded in the local press in a tight column of excited prose. 'A memorable day', the reporter exulted. 'Thousands of people assembled . . . most successful auspices' . . . No wonder 'the inhabitants celebrated with much éclat and the town was en fête'. Much praise was lavished by the reporter on the 'admirable' arrangements of the shipyard foreman, Mr Cass. He lives on, heavily moustached, in a treasured old photograph which also depicts members of the Cochrane family.

Selby, it seemed, offered everything Beverley lacked. And not only would it cost Cochrane's less to receive their materials by rail and water, but completed ships could be delivered 'much more cheaply and expeditiously' – which might seem surprising until you remember the remarkable navigability – bends or no bends – of the Ouse on her way to the Humber. The ship they were launching that day and on which Lady Raincliffe, with ceremony and champagne, bestowed the name *Volta*, was the 216th trawler on the firm's books.

Cochrane's, it was claimed at a celebratory lunch, had already built more steam trawlers than any other company in Great Britain. Yet the operation had not gone entirely without a hitch. Mr Andrew Cochrane, the founder, proposing Lady Raincliffe's health, confessed to having felt 'a little nervous' when *Volta* seemed to hesitate shyly before leaving the stocks. Thanks, finally, to the force with which her ladyship had 'discharged the christening elements', the vessel, confidently expected to be the first of many additions to the fishing fleets of Hull and Grimsby, 'took the water in fine style'

Victorian confidence and exultation filled every heart. And why not? From turning the first sod on the Selby site to the first launch there, only ten months had elapsed, during which extensive work-shops had been built, plant erected and new roads

*Seen through the glass case containing a model of 'Yorkshireman', a tug built at Selby, naval architect Eric Hammal works on further production plans at the Cochrane yard*

*Almost hidden by cables, a worker equips a vessel with its complex 'nervous system'*

made. And yet further expansion was planned! It was proposed to make steam trawlers the yard's speciality and all that was lacking now was housing for their workers.

Had they foreseen the vicissitudes which were to befall Hull's fishing industry, those titled guests and Selby worthies might have been less sanguine. They would certainly have been astonished to see, as I did on the day of my visit, the shell of an oil tanker rearing skyward from the quiet riverside.

Naval architect by profession, Eric Hammal is also the company's unofficial but dedicated archivist. His records show that the company started as Cochrane, Cooper, Hamilton and Schofield. In 1898, the year of the move to Selby, it became Cochrane and Cooper, and despite the earlier date of its origin at Beverley, the official centenary may well be celebrated in 1998.

Andrew Cochrane, the founder, was succeeded in the business by his three sons. But the family connection ended when Lewis Cochrane left in the mid-1960s. By then the firm had been sold to the

Ross Group, of Grimsby, for whom Cochrane's had built fishing vessels for year upon year. Today Cochrane's largely controls its own activities as part of North British Maritime of Hull, which belongs to Howard Smith Industries, a large public company in Australia with marine interests and an eye to Europe.

With a workforce of about three hundred, Cochrane's remains one of the largest employers in Selby. For nearly a hundred years shipbuilding has been a family tradition in the town, sometimes with three generations employed at one time. They have turned out ships in peace and war – fighting ships, such as patrol gun boats and armed trawlers, as well as fishing vessels. In the reception area at Cochrane's offices there is a model of the *Margaret Rose,* 'first cruiser stern trawler to be built at the Cochrane yard, Selby, twice in the 1930s top ship in her class, blown up in the lock pits during the Dunkirk evacuation.'

No doubt many other Cochrane-built vessels have been lost through wartime action, but often their stories have been lost with them, despite Eric Hammal's efforts to record them. During the First World War Cochrane's built a veritable fleet of vessels for the Admiralty – armed trawlers – with a gun mounted for'ard. A continuous stream of enquiries about these and other vessels reaches the company from historians and others, who often supply information eagerly seized upon by Eric for his archives. For example, 'Someone sent us a list of ''Mersey'' Class patrol gun boats built by Cochrane's with details of where these ships were sunk.'

It was the variety of shipping built at Selby that drew Eric Hammal from his native Sunderland, where the main product was tankers and dry cargo vessels. That same variety makes it difficult to generalise about this very complex industry. The first step in a ship's life may indeed be 'no more than a dozen lines' from the customer describing in the briefest detail his requirements – length, draught, approximate tonnage, intended cargo, manning

*Cochrane's shipyard from across the Ouse*

*Above: As orders for new construction improved in the late 1930s the shipyard would often have up to eight vessels being constructed on the building berth, seen here. There is a simple crane derrick for lifting parts onto vessels and a large workforce was required*

levels, speed and preferred type of engine and data on where the ship will operate.

This information becomes the naval architect's brief, and far more is required of him than drawings. It is his task to prepare a full specification of the ship, to enable the price to be calculated. All of which will be submitted to the owner, who will probably receive similar submissions from other ship-builders.

Once an order is received and all the design details settled, the information is passed into the drawing offices, where, in effect, the proposal is 'broken down' into small sections and work begins on hundreds of detailed drawings. Depending on the size of the vessel, this process might take anything from three to six months. Steel and equipment are ordered and, meanwhile, every effort is made to get work under way in the yard and thus keep construction time to a minimum. Templates

have to be made, steel plates must be delivered, bent to the required shape and welded to withstand the rigours of existence on the ever-moving sea.

I am old enough to remember the days when the supposed virtues of rivets, as against welding, were much lauded. The image of the shipyard worker and his mate fearlessly tossing red-hot rivets and catching them in a bucket has its appeal, but rivets now belong as much to the past as the dragon-prowed Viking ships which once sailed up the Ouse to ravish York. 'Rivets leaked', says Eric succinctly. 'When you weld two pieces of steel together they become one. Remember, a ship is a long box. It flexes. You expect a ship to move. Her plates are giving and moving and twisting all the time. And the ship used to give first of all at the rivets: they'd work slack and you'd start getting leakages.' The blend of prosaic realism and unconscious poetry in a north-eastern accent reminds me of sailing in a rolling wartime aircraft carrier and makes me realise what prompted Conrad's pen.

Ships are built in units of perhaps fifteen tons,

under cover at first, before they are lifted out on to the berth alongside the river, where they are assembled. Into the steel shell are fitted engines, gearboxes, generators, pumps, winches, propellers – all supplied by specialist manufacturers dependent and depended upon by the ship-builder. 'So if a shipbuilder goes down, it affects an awful lot of people.' With Eric Hammal I toured the yard, stepping over the network of cables for a great battery of power machinery. Two oil tankers were under construction, though this is acknowledged to be a lean time for the industry.

During the First World War, Admiralty contracts were so urgent that an old photograph shows at least seven pairs of armed trawlers under construction lining the riverside two abreast. During the 1939-45 war the call was more for salvage tugs. With peace came new demands, most notably perhaps for ferries, including the highly sophisticated roll-on roll-off vessels operated by Sealink and Caledonian MacBrayne.

In war or peace Cochrane's meets the challenge, whether for towing ships ranging from Herculean tugs to ocean-going salvage vessels, armed to fight fire or plough through ice, for oil tankers or dry cargo vessels and luxury yachts. 'Just about everything that floats', says Hammal. They leave the riverside yard at Selby in a variety that would astonish the thousands who gathered nearly a century ago to cheer the launch of the *Volta,* first steam trawler ever built at Selby.

*Selby Abbey is framed on the skyline by a gantry while a shipyard worker paints the bridge of a ship nearing completion on the Ouse*

*Right: a view from the bridge*

# At the house of the mouse

## Thompson's craftsmen, Kilburn

Bob Thompson's name and work are known far beyond the boundaries of the Broad Acres. He was surely unique in his day and thanks to successive generations, he remains so. If ever a craftsman made a memorable mark it was the wood carver of Kilburn. And without his signature, the mark of the mouse, no piece of exquisitely finished work, in English oak, leaves the premises of his heirs and successors, Robert Thompson's Craftsmen Limited. Even on the base of a lovely carving of an unsuspecting fox there lurks a cheeky little rodent.

It's surprising (and therefore all the more reassuring) to find that the company's home is still at Kilburn in a timbered cottage, once Bob Thompson's home, that is known as 'The House of the Mouse'. Furthermore, as I was told by Ian Thompson Cartwright, great-grandson of the Mouseman, no two mice are exactly alike. The difference may be no more than an extra curl in the tail, or an unusual angle of ear or whisker, but it's there. Thompson mice are individuals to a mouse, which is just as it should be, for no man was more of an individual than their creator.

Various accounts of the origin of the mouse are in currency, but there's no doubt in my mind that the true one has been told by Thompson himself. Working one day on the furnishing of a church, he heard one of his workmen complain that he and his colleagues were 'as poor as church mice'. Almost unconsciously, and no doubt hiding a smile beneath his moustache, Thompson found himself carving a mouse on the work in hand. Neither he nor the mouse had any idea in those days just how vast a family it would father or how far afield they would travel.

Beneath centuries-old beams I talked to Ian about the heritage left by his forebear to Kilburn and the world; the business is today a flourishing memorial to the village's own great craftsman. 'It certainly wouldn't be the same', agreed Ian in his thoughtful, North Riding way, 'if it were on an industrial site.'

Kilburn, with its hilarious summertime 'Feast and Local Costume Frolics' and its beloved White

*Above: the library at Ampleforth College*

*The White Horse of Kilburn on Roulston Scar in the background; in the foreground is timber seasoning for Thompson's craftsmen near Robert Thompson's former home, now the company HQ*

Horse landmark emblazoned on Roulston Scar, has been aptly dubbed 'a village of schoolboys' – and for a variety of reasons not necessarily connected with Thompson. Schoolboys there are in plenty hereabouts, for only seven miles from Kilburn is Ampleforth College, one of the most famous Roman Catholic schools in England, where the library is so much a Thompson memorial that he himself called it 'my room'. Well he might, for he had worked on it for about thirty years. He had good reason to love Ampleforth, for the Benedictine monks, who serve both school and abbey, were among his first customers. While he was still unknown and struggling, they commissioned him to make an oak cross for the churchyard.

As a young man working in his father's workshop at Kilburn on all the jobs that fell to a village carpenter's lot, he dreamed of emulating the ancient craftsmen who beautified churches with their marvellous carving in English oak. It was the headmaster of Ampleforth, Father Paul Nevill, who, recognising Thompson's genius, commissioned him to provide furniture for the college.

Thus began the Thompson tradition which is continued by the present craftsmen. The workshop is closed to the public from April to October. The showroom, which has more the air of a gallery, is open all the year round, and when I visited it on a mellow, sunlit day there was a steady trickle of customers through the rooms – quiet, smiling people. They are natural clients for what Bob Thompson once said his 'mouse' represented – 'industry in quiet places . . . a mouse manages to scrape and chew away at the hardest wood', he said. 'I thought that was maybe like this workshop'. How right he was, and how aptly the little rodent still symbolises the quiet zeal of Robert Thomson's Craftsmen. Contrary to the frantic philosophy of so many businesses today, selling seems secondary at the House of the Mouse and for that reason, perhaps, it is all the more successful.

This is a company, with no advertising budget. It hardly needs one with an army of silently industrious mice as its sales force. Anyway, what need had Thompson to advertise when a letter posted in America and addressed simply to 'The Mouseman, England' reached him safely?

As Ian Cartwright explained, the workshop is technically a factory, and therefore as subject to all the legal responsibilities of a factory as the premises of ICI. 'In the quieter months we can cope with people wandering around. But we were getting coachloads of people, sometimes sixty at a time. We're responsible for everybody in the workshop. It's a problem that's always increasing.' Furthermore, as he frankly admitted, 'We can't afford to pay men just to chat to tourists'.

One way in which the firm hopes to cope with the problem is to open a working museum across the road from the 'factory' (the word hardly fits), in the original workshop. A blacksmith's shop and an ever-growing store of memorabilia are ready and waiting for incorporation into what will surely become one of the most popular attractions of the North York Moors.

The production workforce – craftsmen and apprentices – numbering thirty, gives the impression of an extended family. Ian Cartwright joined the business on leaving school. He still revels in working with wood, but having to look after thirty men and over three hundred customers can severely

limit his choice in the matter.

I asked him where Thompson's Craftsmen differed most noticeably from other concerns in a similar business. His answer, 'Our emphasis is on quality rather than quantity', may have seemed predictable, but it was none the less a simple statement of fact. One advantage of their comparatively large size is the ability to be selective in their choice of timber, carried in quite large quantities, as demonstrated by the stacks of oak planks seasoning in the open air around the works. 'With such large stocks', Ian explains, 'We can pick and choose any particular tree for a particular job. Smaller, one-man concerns may only have the timber that is immediately to hand, no matter what job they need it for.'

Thompson's buy oak from many parts of the country – from the north of Scotland to the south coast. A good oak tree is 250 years a-growing, so a company such as Thompson's is happy to buy good timber where it can – on the Castle Howard estate

*Carved open-weave chair backs await assembly*

*Tea break!*

near York, maybe, or at Bramham Park, near Wetherby. Securing adequate stocks gets no easier with the passing of time. 'People are now much more concerned about trees being cut down than they were thirty years ago', says Ian. 'Nowadays the estates have replanting programmes for putting the hardwoods back in, but that's hardly likely to help me in my lifetime.' Will stocks be sufficient for the foreseeable future? 'We're a forward-looking company', he says, 'We're buying timber this back-end that we'll be using in five or six years time.'

No shortage of timber at the moment, then, but surprisingly perhaps, there is a shortage of apprentices. Ian attributes this to the emphasis in present-day education on academic subjects rather than craftwork. Computer technology, is studied at the expense of such subjects as woodwork, metalwork, pottery, basket-making or weaving – 'Yet we all

need chairs to sit on and pots to drink from'.

Even so, he has observed that while at one time people would prefer cheap, machine-made articles to a traditional hand-made piece that would last several lifetimes, this trend, happily, is now being reversed. He attributes this partly to the arts and crafts revival but also to a naturally developing appreciation of excellence nourished by the current interest in antiques and the encouragement in recent years of rural crafts. 'After all, that's how the majority of people used to earn their living in this country.' Indeed much of Thompson's success could be attributed to their desire to work with the best materials using the best methods. During a tour of the workshops I hardly saw a nail. Instead, perfect dovetail and mortice and tenon joints and skilfully angled dowels are used. Plywood, you might think, had never been invented: 'Everything is from solid wood – drawer bottoms, back panels. And it's always well finished, right the way through.'

To maintain quality in their work, whoever starts

a task takes it to its conclusion. 'It's one man's work, which is reflected in the finished piece.' As for design, here again the Mouseman lives on with surprising vigour, for many of the articles now being made follow the lines of his originals or are variations upon them. 'Robert Thompson', says his great-grandson, 'introduced the octagonal and Gothic styles embodied in the furniture we now produce. In the sixties we tried some contemporary designs but the idea was an absolute flop. People who came to see us want to buy Robert Thompson-style furniture. At least the experiment wasn't a complete waste of time, because we learnt that we should stick to what we know best.'

And what they learned a long time ago is that traditionally-made oak furniture is practically indestructible. In its finished state it conveys an

*Left: planning an owl*

*Centre: the art of the adze*

*Right: sandpapering a chair back*

impression of strength and elegance, of timelessness and permanence. As you watch its construction under the hands of a dedicated craftsmen you hesitate to intrude on his concentration. Could anything be further from the doctrine of 'built-in' obsolescence' which decrees a short and shoddy life for so many of today's products?

There seems to be no likelihood that Thompson's will run out of orders or that their present products will lose their appeal. Nevertheless, the occasional new design is introduced where an opening presents itself. Recent additions to the standard range include a cocktail cabinet and a small writing desk. But too many such innovations could be self-defeating. As Ian Cartwright points out: 'We make over a hundred standard items; we have a workforce of thirty and a waiting list of sixteen-to-eighteen months, with over three hundred customers on our books at one time. So to start introducing more pieces tends to put everything else further and further behind. As things stand at present, we feel we can offer people a good, sound, complete range of furniture and we are very happy with that.'

To each craftsman one apprentice is assigned. Occasionally there is a clash of personalities and then adjustments must be made. Always care is taken to ensure the continuing development of the youth as a craftsman, to the ultimate benefit of the work and to all concerned.

Apprentices, who must first and foremost demonstrate a keen interest in the work, are initially engaged for a three-month trial period, in the full knowledge that early enthusiasm may wax or wane or dry up altogether. Good starters may prove disappointing or slow beginners blossom in due time, to become truly a part of the Thompson 'family' and stay with it, as some have done, for fifty years. 'Age-ism' has no place in the Thompson philosophy. It is recognised that advancing years need signal no loss of skill. On the contrary such experience is invaluable.

There are more than monetary rewards for the craftsman. 'A one-off job can be a work of art', says Ian, 'a memorial to the man who made it, because that particular article may never be repeated by us.' Examples of such 'one-offs' include the reredos [ornamental screen at the back of the altar] for a Wordsworth chapel at Ambleside, a memorial font for a church in York and a board to commemorate the origin of a county cricket club in Durham. The craftsman entrusted with the memorial to such an historic event in the world of sport was 'a cricket fanatic', Ian explained. 'That's how we apportion the work, suiting the task to fit the flair of the craftsman engaged on it – and everybody gets a change round. And there's no job card saying the job must be finished in a given number of hours. Admittedly, some are fast workers, some are slower, but at the end of the day things even out,'

There is nothing precious about the Thompson policy, which combines a determined pursuit of excellence with hard-headed common-sense. Tools, for instance, are chosen for their suitability, not for their antiquity. 'We use machines for roughing-out', says Ian. 'Even Robert Thompson, before the war, had machinery. We even have a smaller workforce now than he had. He employed over forty men, as against our thirty.'

There is one ancient tool, beloved of the medieval craftsmen, and admired by Thompson, that shapes much of the work produced at Kilburn. It is the

*Evolution of a Thompson mouse*
*Right: mice in waiting*

adze, the long-handled implement with its blade set at right angles to the shaft, which was swung by shipwrights and others in roughing-out and squaring the timbers of ships or houses. Used here to much more delicate effect, the adze is almost as synonymous with Thompson as his mouse. This is the tool used to give the silky, gently undulating effect – as English as the oak itself – to the surfaces of much Thompson furniture.

The destination of a finished piece is the fuming room, where ammonia is used to give the oak the desired tinge of greenish gold. At one time the same effect was achieved by hanging it in the stables! Last of all comes the anointing with beeswax.

Ask Ian his title and he'll say 'general dogsbody', for this family-run business is not 'into' titles. What counts at Kilburn is getting on with the job in hand and 'doing the best we can. If there's something to do, whether it's sweeping the floor or making coffee for a guest, we get on and do it.' What jobs stay in his mind as triumphs or disasters? No disasters, apparently, which is not as unbelievable as it might sound. Such is their pride that: 'If we're not happy with a job, it's stopped.' Triumphs are easy to recall, Ian has particularly happy memories of regimental work, such as that for the Royal Corps of Signals at Catterick. And, of course, the work at Ampleforth, which embodies so much Thompson family history and inspires the sense of tradition: 'I can go to work there in the 1990s and see something made by one of my family in the 1920s.'

At this rate, in a hundred years hence another Thompson-trained craftsman might be making a very similar statement and nothing will have changed except the dates.

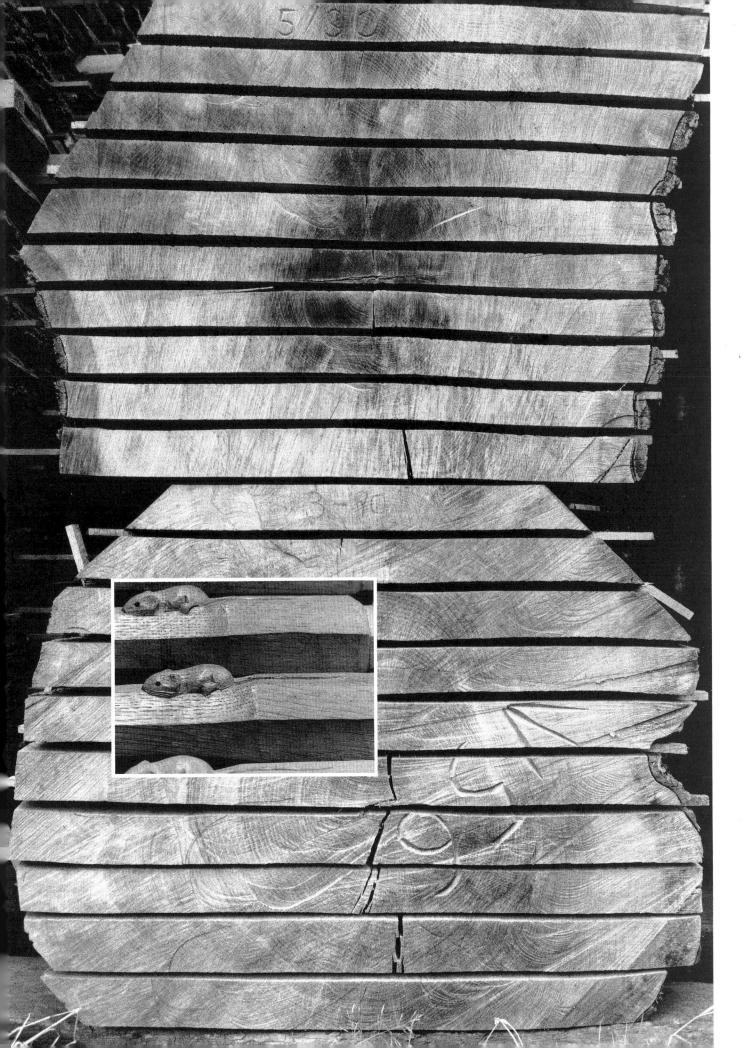

# The cheese the monks made

fine cheese from Wensleydale

When I began writing this book, the making of Wensleydale cheese, produced since medieval times in the dale whose name it bears, seemed securely based in Hawes. For generations it had been a source of jobs as well as pride in this Dales metropolis. Then, weeks after I had toured the creamery, where the enthusiasm of the workforce was almost tangible, the owners, Dairy Crest (registered office in Surrey), announced that the Hawes creamery was to close.

The immediate impact was shattering. Residents saw the decision as little less than a death sentence on Hawes, which would be denuded of its young inhabitants due to a lack of jobs. Rumours that production was to be transferred to Longridge in Lancashire did nothing to soften the blow.

But the cheese which had survived the restrictions imposed by wartime bureaucracy does not die easily. Local businessmen lost no time in launching a rescue operation. Local initiatives, we were told, were 'exploring possibilities' of starting up the creamery again in Hawes, perhaps even on the same site. There was talk of using money from wealthy county exiles to save the industry. One thing above all was demonstrated: Yorkshire cares about its famous cheese and the dale that produced it.

'There are all sorts of possibilities', I was told by Peter Annison, chairman of Hawes Chamber of Trade. 'We've had tremendous offers of support, and we're very determined.'

By the time these words are printed we may know whether Wensleydale cheese will continue to be produced in Hawes or whether, like so many other traditional British cheeses, it will be made far from the place where it originated centuries ago . . .

The Cistercian brothers of Jervaulx Abbey in Wensleydale were concerned with more than prayer. They were famous, for instance, for the horses they bred and no less so for the cheese they made from the milk of moorland ewes. Wensleydale cheese is no longer made from sheeps' milk but tradition holds that it was the monks' recipes, left behind when Henry VIII drove them from their beautifully sited abbey, that gave rise to an industry which became integral to the life and folklore of the dale.

It has had a chequered history. As long ago as 1898, Edward Chapman, a successful Hawes corn and provision merchant, had founded a creamery at Hawes and begun making cheese in factory conditions. Mr Chapman made excellent cheese and his creamery prospered, until both his sons were carried off by the influenza epidemic of 1918. Then, his heart broken, he sold the business.

From then on it had a number of owners, and eventually, in the mid-thirties, ran into difficulties from which it was saved when Kit Calvert, in Hawes market place, rallied the local farmers to mount a rescue. Before long, he was managing director of the new enterprise. The war brought its changes and challenges, but with the return of peace, Wensleydale creameries expanded rapidly and when retirement age was looming, Kit sold the business to the Milk Marketing Board for half a million pounds. He would buy a pony and trap, he said, and spend his retirement driving around the lanes of his native dale.

Kit Calvert, who built the Hawes creamery which was until recently owned by the J M Nuttall group, a division of Dairy Crest, has been justly called 'the King of Wensleydale'. Farmer, dialect expert and, in his later years, a quirky bookseller, he was famous far beyond Hawes. Kit is credited with the post-war revival of the cheese industry, which had dwindled after wartime rationing regulations reduced a cheese, once the prize-winning pride of many a Dales farmer's wife, to 'third' or 'fourth' grade, because of its high moisture content and low acidity.

Sadly, Kit is no longer here to be interviewed, but he has more than once told how 'all hell was let loose' in the dale over the edict that more moisture must come out of the cheese and more acidity be introduced. The cheesemakers had only two choices – either to concur or to allow their milk to be collected

*Grazing cattle in the dale of Wensleydale*

*Inset: real Wensleydale Cheese*

by the Board's tankers (which incidentally saved them money, since the price was good and they laid out less on wages in the dairy). Cheesemaking continued, but under conditions imposed by wartime regulations defining a 'Grade 1' cheese. When the war ended, and, with it, rationing, the Milk Marketing Board like everyone else hoped that the traditional Wensleydale cheese would return, together with many other longed-for delights of peacetime. Representatives of the Board arrived in Hawes to persuade Kit to take them to meet the 176 registered Wensleydale cheesemakers and ask them to resume their cheesemaking in the pre-war way. But all too often the old skill had rusted from lack of use, while both consumers and shopkeepers had almost forgotten what the old cheese really tasted like. The old way, it seemed, had gone forever, and even if it hadn't, the introduction of pasteurization, which destroys the natural bacteria, would have sealed its fate.

But it takes more than wartime regulations and restrictions to kill off a cheese like Wensleydale.

There had to be change though, it was too much to expect that Wensleydale would forever be made from ewes' milk (average yield during the milking season a pint a day). It was inevitable that some day the thermometer would replace the testing elbow of the farmer's wife and her kitchen would give way to the factory.

Ian Millward, formerly creamery manager at Hawes, describing the unique appeal of Wensleydale cheese, talked of its famous 'honeyed' flavour and stressed that this is a cheese that demands to be eaten fresh, ideally at three or four weeks old.

Colour, as well as taste, is an important characteristic of Wensleydale. It is the high chalk content of Wensleydale grazing land that imparts its famous whiteness to the cheese. 'In Wensleydale', said Ian, 'some cheesemakers were so expert that they could even tell which side of a hill had the most chalk.'

*Pushing back the Wensleydale curd (above), prior to running off the whey (right)*

Cheese has been not only his occupation but a food he enjoys. Not surprising, then, that one of the pleasures of his job was the selection of cheeses for entry in shows, at which Hawes creamery has certainly had its fair share of winners. A wall of his office was emblazoned with certificates testifying to high awards gained in many parts of the country, including the two main cheese shows, the Nantwich international event and the Bath and West at Shepton Mallet. Nor was the creamery's success limited to Wensleydale cheese, though this was its principle product.

Other fine cheeses, including Cheshire, Lancashire, Double Gloucester, Red Leicester and the popular Sage Derby, have been made at Hawes, as well as one other which, like their principle product Wensleydale, might be considered indigenous. It was also developed at Hawes creamery, and given the name Emmerdale in honour of the popular Dales serial on Yorkshire Television. The name was chosen by Ian's predecessor, Richard Davies and the then company secretary, the late Miss Betty Lyne. Emmerdale cheese, said Ian, a hard, rich-flavoured cheese, which caused delight in Hawes by winning a first prize against much longer-established products from other creameries.

Wensleydale cheese production has inevitably changed since the time of the monks, what follows is a description of the processes followed at Hawes creamery while it was still in full production.

Milk arrived at Hawes by tanker and was tested for quality before pasteurization. This process involved heating the milk to 72 degrees centigrade for fifteen seconds, after which it was cooled to 30 degrees and pumped to one of seven 4,500-litre vats. There it was inoculated with a starter and there the cheesemaking process really began.

The starter was a mixture of specific bacteria produced under stringent conditions in the creamery's lab. These bacteria were in a sense the vital first workers in the manufacturing process, because part of their role was to impart the actual flavour of the cheese. When the milk in the vat had reached the required acidity level, the enzyme known as rennett was added. This caused the milk to coagulate. Then, in an open-topped vat, rotating knives cut the curd

Left: cutting and turning Wensleydale curd

Above: milling, or grinding, the salted Wensleydale curd prior to filling cheese moulds

Below: filling moulds of Wensleydale curd, which are then subjected to high pressure to ensure that the curd takes the shape of the mould

into small cubes and separated the curds from the residual liquid, the whey. Further moisture was removed from the curd particles by steam heat, which also increased the acidity.

After the whey had been drained off, the blocks of curd were turned at intervals and piled to allow the particles to fuse together and assume the texture we all recognise as that of cheese. All the while, acidity was increasing and when this had reached the required level, the curd, after salting, was put through a mill which reduced the acid development. The curd was packed into moulds, weighed and pre-pressed before being taken to the press room and subjected overnight to high pressures which ensured that the curd took the shape of the mould. Cheesemaking, still largely a stranger to automation and mechanisation, depends very much on the skill that is acquired with experience; on an almost instinctive awareness, for instance, of how much and how often to turn the curd, depending on the time of year or the 'set' of a particular curd.

From the press room the cheeses went to the packing room, where traditional cheeses were

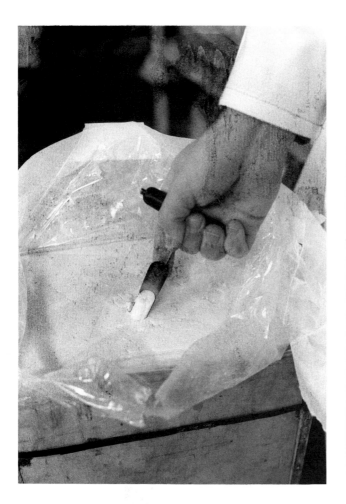

placed on shelves, there to remain for up to three days to allow the surface to become dry. A protective coating was applied to seal them from the atmosphere. This not only prevented contamination but stopped weight loss by evaporation.

In the cheese store, where the temperature was maintained at about ten degrees centigrade, the cheeses were allowed to mature on shelves, while being regularly subjected to quality checks. Maturation periods varied according to the types of cheese. Wensleydale was normally matured for two to three weeks before being dispatched.

'We try to retain the traditional characteristics of our cheeses as much as possible', said Ian Millward, when I toured the creamery with him shortly before it closed. 'There's always a danger that a product can become just another cheese.' He felt success had been achieved when tourists from other areas said, 'We just can't get cheese like this – why can't we?' Often these visitors had bought their cheese at its freshest in local shops, but the creamery had also an expanding trade with multiple stores (as well as a

*Left: samples of cheese for testing are obtained by means of the 'iron', which is plunged into the body of the cheese, in this case a first-class block of Wensleydale*

*Above: other cheeses, besides Wensleydale, have been made at Hawes. Here, husband and wife team Dennis and Margaret Fawcett cut and pack traditional Double Gloucester and Red Leicester*

healthy export market, particularly in Canada and the USA).

'People are always on the look-out for good traditional cheese', said Ian. Furthermore, new cheeses, sometimes from small makers, are always coming up on to the market and we have to make sure that we compete. Continental cheeses, too, attract interest now that people are becoming more adventurous in their eating.'

The best way to eat a Wensleydale cheese? 'As quickly as possible', says Ian Millward, and although he said it with a smile, there was no doubt what he meant: for with the native cheese of Wensleydale, freshness is all. 'Buy it regularly in the quantities you can eat in a short time, rather than buying a big piece and trying to keep it.' If you're

*Wensleydale 'Sovereign' cheeses*

from Yorkshire you already know the answer to the next question: what to eat with your Wensleydale? apple pie, of course, or at the festive season, with Christmas cake.

As for what to drink with Wensleydale, the wine list is long enough to suit most palates: try Orvieta, Italian dry white, rosé, Laski Reisling, German fruity wine or a fruit wine such as redcurrant.

If you like, you can cook with Wensleydale. The English Cheese Council can give you four recipes. But if you overcook, you'll probably ruin the soft texture.

There was an air of optimism in Hawes then which may well reappear in the course of time. I, for one, certainly hope it will. Many of the sixty or so workers formerly employed at the Wensleydale creamery surely inherited skills from their forerunners in past centuries, and at least one of the former personnel was himself the son of a cheesemaker. Watching and talking to the men and studying their always demanding tasks, you sensed their pride in the product. And a well-founded pride it was, as those show certificates in Ian's office – often won against much bigger creameries – amply testified.

Long may it flourish!

*The ruins of Jervaulx Abbey, where the Wensleydale cheesemaking tradition began*